CHINESE NAMES, SURNAM
LOCATIONS & ADDRESSES
中国大陆地址集

FUJIAN PROVINCE - PART 10
福建省

ZIYUE TANG
汤子玥

1

ACKNOWLEDGEMENT

I am deeply indebted to my friends and family members to support me throughout my life. Without their invaluable love and guidance, this work wouldn't have been possible.

Thank you

Ziyue Tang

汤子玥

PREFACE

The book introduces foreigner students to the Chinese names along with locations and addresses from the **Fujian** Province of China (中国福建省). The book contains 150 entries (names, addresses) explained with simplified Chinese characters, pinyin and English.

Chinese names follow the standard convention where the given name is written after the surname. For example, in 王威 (Wang Wei), Wang is the surname, and Wei is the given name. Further, the surnames are generally made of one (王) or two characters (司马). Similarly, the given names are also made of either one or two characters. For example, 司马威 (Sima Wei) is a three character Chinese name suitable for men. 司马威威 is a four character Chinese name.

Chinese addresses are comprised of different administrative units that start with the largest geographic entity (country) and continue to the smallest entity (county, building names, room number). For example, a typical address in Nanjing city (capital of Jiangsu province) would look like 江苏省南京市清华路 28 栋 520 室 (Jiāngsū shěng nánjīng shì qīnghuá lù 28 dòng 520 shì; Room 520, Building 28, Qinghua Road, Nanjing City, Jiangsu Province).

CONTENTS

CHAPTER 1: NAME, SURNAME & ADDRESSES (1-30)

1351。姓名: 蓝沛居

住址（酒店）：福建省龙岩市新罗区谢惟路 352 号超秀酒店（邮政编码：961295）。联系电话：29869659。电子邮箱：fcwgh@ejcdlvoi.biz.cn

Zhù zhǐ: Lán Bèi Jū Fújiàn Shěng Lóngyán Shì Xīn Luō Qū Xiè Wéi Lù 352 Hào Chāo Xiù Jiǔ Diàn (Yóuzhèng Biānmǎ：961295). Liánxì Diànhuà：29869659. Diànzǐ Yóuxiāng：fcwgh@ejcdlvoi.biz.cn

Bei Ju Lan, Chao Xiu Hotel, 352 Xie Wei Road, Silla District, Longyan, Fujian. Postal Code: 961295. Phone Number：29869659. E-mail：fcwgh@ejcdlvoi.biz.cn

1352。姓名: 尤振进

住址（公共汽车站）：福建省漳州市华安县威发路 571 号国翼站（邮政编码：608395）。联系电话：86020939。电子邮箱：fdgwe@wfsqizke.transport.cn

Zhù zhǐ: Yóu Zhèn Jìn Fújiàn Shěng Zhāngzhōu Shì Huáānxiàn Wēi Fā Lù 571 Hào Guó Yì Zhàn (Yóuzhèng Biānmǎ：608395). Liánxì Diànhuà：86020939. Diànzǐ Yóuxiāng：fdgwe@wfsqizke.transport.cn

Zhen Jin You, Guo Yi Bus Station, 571 Wei Fa Road, Huaan County, Zhangzhou, Fujian. Postal Code: 608395. Phone Number：86020939. E-mail：fdgwe@wfsqizke.transport.cn

1353。姓名: 佘铭钦

住址（公园）：福建省泉州市德化县斌阳路 277 号坡宝公园（邮政编码：316061）。联系电话：11859821。电子邮箱：edqfr@sqczebto.parks.cn

Zhù zhǐ: Shé Míng Qīn Fújiàn Shěng Quánzhōu Shì Dé Huà Xiàn Bīn Yáng Lù 277 Hào Pō Bǎo Gōng Yuán (Yóuzhèng Biānmǎ：316061). Liánxì Diànhuà：11859821. Diànzǐ Yóuxiāng：edqfr@sqczebto.parks.cn

Ming Qin She, Po Bao Park, 277 Bin Yang Road, Dehua County, Quanzhou, Fujian. Postal Code: 316061. Phone Number：11859821. E-mail：edqfr@sqczebto.parks.cn

1354。姓名: 赏骥易

住址（博物院）：福建省厦门市海沧区友南路 682 号厦门博物馆（邮政编码：867826）。联系电话：59519868。电子邮箱：agkvw@ucrebzjf.museums.cn

Zhù zhǐ: Shǎng Jì Yì Fújiàn Shěng Xiàmén Shì Hǎi Cāng Qū Yǒu Nán Lù 682 Hào Xiàmén Bó Wù Guǎn (Yóuzhèng Biānmǎ：867826). Liánxì Diànhuà：59519868. Diànzǐ Yóuxiāng：agkvw@ucrebzjf.museums.cn

Ji Yi Shang, Xiamen Museum, 682 You Nan Road, Haicang District, Xiamen, Fujian. Postal Code: 867826. Phone Number：59519868. E-mail：agkvw@ucrebzjf.museums.cn

1355。姓名: 纪铁红

住址（酒店）：福建省平潭综合实验区平潭县龙化路 607 号全黎酒店（邮政编码：345630）。联系电话：98520215。电子邮箱：zdvkq@vojemhsr.biz.cn

Zhù zhǐ: Jì Tiě Hóng Fújiàn Shěng Píng Tán Zònghé Shíyàn Qū Píng Tán Xiàn Lóng Huā Lù 607 Hào Quán Lí Jiǔ Diàn (Yóuzhèng Biānmǎ：345630). Liánxì Diànhuà：98520215. Diànzǐ Yóuxiāng：zdvkq@vojemhsr.biz.cn

Tie Hong Ji, Quan Li Hotel, 607 Long Hua Road, Pingtan County, Pingtan Comprehensive Experimental Area, Fujian. Postal Code: 345630. Phone Number：98520215. E-mail：zdvkq@vojemhsr.biz.cn

1356。姓名: 柯智盛

住址（酒店）：福建省厦门市思明区德舟路 703 号帆铁酒店（邮政编码：145052）。联系电话：19481730。电子邮箱：knqom@sepdyfzt.biz.cn

Zhù zhǐ: Kē Zhì Chéng Fújiàn Shěng Xiàmén Shì Sī Míng Qū Dé Zhōu Lù 703 Hào Fān Tiě Jiǔ Diàn (Yóuzhèng Biānmǎ：145052). Liánxì Diànhuà：19481730. Diànzǐ Yóuxiāng：knqom@sepdyfzt.biz.cn

Zhi Cheng Ke, Fan Tie Hotel, 703 De Zhou Road, Siming District, Xiamen, Fujian. Postal Code: 145052. Phone Number：19481730. E-mail：knqom@sepdyfzt.biz.cn

1357。姓名: 樊骥迅

住址（家庭）：福建省泉州市惠安县冕领路 637 号土亚公寓 31 层 197 室（邮政编码：395534）。联系电话：73273075。电子邮箱：tjkwn@hdbugjmw.cn

Zhù zhǐ: Fán Jì Xùn Fújiàn Shěng Quánzhōu Shì Huìānxiàn Miǎn Lǐng Lù 637 Hào Tǔ Yà Gōng Yù 31 Céng 197 Shì (Yóuzhèng Biānmǎ：395534). Liánxì Diànhuà：73273075. Diànzǐ Yóuxiāng：tjkwn@hdbugjmw.cn

Ji Xun Fan, Room# 197, Floor# 31, Tu Ya Apartment, 637 Mian Ling Road, Huian County, Quanzhou, Fujian. Postal Code: 395534. Phone Number：73273075. E-mail：tjkwn@hdbugjmw.cn

1358。姓名: 齐土辉

住址（湖泊）：福建省漳州市华安县化化路 393 号稼晖湖（邮政编码：214099）。联系电话：98425230。电子邮箱：miowl@zblthnvr.lakes.cn

Zhù zhǐ: Qí Tǔ Huī Fújiàn Shěng Zhāngzhōu Shì Huáānxiàn Huà Huà Lù 393 Hào Jià Huī Hú (Yóuzhèng Biānmǎ：214099). Liánxì Diànhuà：98425230. Diànzǐ Yóuxiāng：miowl@zblthnvr.lakes.cn

Tu Hui Qi, Jia Hui Lake, 393 Hua Hua Road, Huaan County, Zhangzhou, Fujian. Postal Code: 214099. Phone Number：98425230. E-mail：miowl@zblthnvr.lakes.cn

1359。姓名: 商可科

住址（湖泊）：福建省漳州市东山县土立路 638 号愈员湖（邮政编码：891577）。联系电话：21916452。电子邮箱：houye@hzauynlr.lakes.cn

Zhù zhǐ: Shāng Kě Kē Fújiàn Shěng Zhāngzhōu Shì Dōngshān Xiàn Tǔ Lì Lù 638 Hào Yù Yuán Hú (Yóuzhèng Biānmǎ：891577). Liánxì Diànhuà：21916452. Diànzǐ Yóuxiāng：houye@hzauynlr.lakes.cn

Ke Ke Shang, Yu Yuan Lake, 638 Tu Li Road, Dongshan County, Zhangzhou, Fujian. Postal Code: 891577. Phone Number：21916452. E-mail：houye@hzauynlr.lakes.cn

1360。姓名: 琴大渊

住址（家庭）：福建省莆田市仙游县坡黎路 974 号员翼公寓 16 层 370 室（邮政编码：980468）。联系电话：17107331。电子邮箱：dqayb@jblaqeyu.cn

Zhù zhǐ: Qín Dài Yuān Fújiàn Shěng Pútián Shì Xiān Yóu Xiàn Pō Lí Lù 974 Hào Yún Yì Gōng Yù 16 Céng 370 Shì (Yóuzhèng Biānmǎ：980468). Liánxì Diànhuà：17107331. Diànzǐ Yóuxiāng：dqayb@jblaqeyu.cn

Dai Yuan Qin, Room# 370, Floor# 16, Yun Yi Apartment, 974 Po Li Road, Xianyou County, Putian, Fujian. Postal Code: 980468. Phone Number：17107331. E-mail：dqayb@jblaqeyu.cn

1361。姓名: 简钢坚

住址（湖泊）：福建省宁德市蕉城区计领路 330 号自茂湖（邮政编码：286600）。联系电话：27048015。电子邮箱：qwcgf@hoqntlfm.lakes.cn

Zhù zhǐ: Jiǎn Gāng Jiān Fújiàn Shěng Níngdé Shì Jiāo Chéngqū Jì Lǐng Lù 330 Hào Zì Mào Hú (Yóuzhèng Biānmǎ：286600). Liánxì Diànhuà：27048015. Diànzǐ Yóuxiāng：qwcgf@hoqntlfm.lakes.cn

Gang Jian Jian, Zi Mao Lake, 330 Ji Ling Road, Jiaocheng District, Ningde, Fujian. Postal Code: 286600. Phone Number： 27048015. E-mail： qwcgf@hoqntlfm.lakes.cn

1362。姓名: 酆奎己

住址（医院）：福建省莆田市城厢区郁仓路 252 号仲跃医院（邮政编码：127209）。联系电话：27402985。电子邮箱：lteqc@aenwmubj.health.cn

Zhù zhǐ: Fēng Kuí Jǐ Fújiàn Shěng Pútián Shì Chéngxiāng Qū Yù Cāng Lù 252 Hào Zhòng Yuè Yī Yuàn (Yóuzhèng Biānmǎ： 127209). Liánxì Diànhuà： 27402985. Diànzǐ Yóuxiāng： lteqc@aenwmubj.health.cn

Kui Ji Feng, Zhong Yue Hospital, 252 Yu Cang Road, Chengxiang District, Putian, Fujian. Postal Code: 127209. Phone Number： 27402985. E-mail： lteqc@aenwmubj.health.cn

1363。姓名: 冷大翰

住址（湖泊）：福建省平潭综合实验区平潭县桥源路 818 号臻祥湖（邮政编码：647882）。联系电话：44118927。电子邮箱：gukam@wqmnsbkp.lakes.cn

Zhù zhǐ: Lěng Dài Hàn Fújiàn Shěng Píng Tán Zònghé Shíyàn Qū Píng Tán Xiàn Qiáo Yuán Lù 818 Hào Zhēn Xiáng Hú (Yóuzhèng Biānmǎ： 647882). Liánxì Diànhuà： 44118927. Diànzǐ Yóuxiāng： gukam@wqmnsbkp.lakes.cn

Dai Han Leng, Zhen Xiang Lake, 818 Qiao Yuan Road, Pingtan County, Pingtan Comprehensive Experimental Area, Fujian. Postal Code: 647882. Phone Number： 44118927. E-mail： gukam@wqmnsbkp.lakes.cn

1364。姓名: 巢福沛

住址（湖泊）：福建省莆田市涵江区冕土路 363 号伦珏湖（邮政编码：635562）。联系电话：55223533。电子邮箱：yoxcp@gembysqk.lakes.cn

Zhù zhǐ: Cháo Fú Pèi Fújiàn Shěng Pútián Shì Hánjiāng Qū Miǎn Tǔ Lù 363 Hào Lún Jué Hú（Yóuzhèng Biānmǎ：635562). Liánxì Diànhuà：55223533. Diànzǐ Yóuxiāng：yoxcp@gembysqk.lakes.cn

Fu Pei Chao, Lun Jue Lake, 363 Mian Tu Road, Hanjiang District, Putian, Fujian. Postal Code: 635562. Phone Number：55223533. E-mail：yoxcp@gembysqk.lakes.cn

1365。姓名: 戴陆豪

住址（家庭）：福建省福州市闽侯县毅浩路 425 号亚跃公寓 1 层 746 室（邮政编码：302572）。联系电话：93797108。电子邮箱：nmexi@bmwjrflz.cn

Zhù zhǐ: Dài Liù Háo Fújiàn Shěng Fúzhōu Shì Mǐn Hóu Xiàn Yì Hào Lù 425 Hào Yà Yuè Gōng Yù 1 Céng 746 Shì (Yóuzhèng Biānmǎ：302572). Liánxì Diànhuà：93797108. Diànzǐ Yóuxiāng：nmexi@bmwjrflz.cn

Liu Hao Dai, Room# 746, Floor# 1, Ya Yue Apartment, 425 Yi Hao Road, Minhou County, Fuzhou, Fujian. Postal Code: 302572. Phone Number：93797108. E-mail：nmexi@bmwjrflz.cn

1366。姓名: 翟发亭

住址（公共汽车站）：福建省三明市建宁县跃兆路 442 号翰不站（邮政编码：256328）。联系电话：74938960。电子邮箱：dawcp@bvaotdku.transport.cn

Zhù zhǐ: Zhái Fā Tíng Fújiàn Shěng Sānmíng Shì Jiàn Níngxiàn Yuè Zhào Lù 442 Hào Hàn Bù Zhàn（Yóuzhèng Biānmǎ：256328). Liánxì Diànhuà：74938960. Diànzǐ Yóuxiāng：dawcp@bvaotdku.transport.cn

Fa Ting Zhai, Han Bu Bus Station, 442 Yue Zhao Road, Jianning County, Sanming, Fujian. Postal Code: 256328. Phone Number：74938960. E-mail：dawcp@bvaotdku.transport.cn

1367。姓名: 车立豪

住址（公司）：福建省南平市建阳区涛楚路 329 号鸣宝有限公司（邮政编码：369915）。联系电话：19034963。电子邮箱：jzfcb@djmsiolk.biz.cn

Zhù zhǐ: Chē Lì Háo Fújiàn Shěng Nánpíng Shì Jiàn Yáng Qū Tāo Chǔ Lù 329 Hào Míng Bǎo Yǒuxiàn Gōngsī (Yóuzhèng Biānmǎ：369915). Liánxì Diànhuà：19034963. Diànzǐ Yóuxiāng：jzfcb@djmsiolk.biz.cn

Li Hao Che, Ming Bao Corporation, 329 Tao Chu Road, Jianyang District, Nanping, Fujian. Postal Code: 369915. Phone Number：19034963. E-mail：jzfcb@djmsiolk.biz.cn

1368。姓名：冷辙国

住址（酒店）：福建省龙岩市新罗区坡骥路 362 号愈征酒店（邮政编码：364452）。联系电话：18017292。电子邮箱：bzdqf@xmrzfpje.biz.cn

Zhù zhǐ: Lěng Zhé Guó Fújiàn Shěng Lóngyán Shì Xīn Luō Qū Pō Jì Lù 362 Hào Yù Zhēng Jiǔ Diàn (Yóuzhèng Biānmǎ：364452). Liánxì Diànhuà：18017292. Diànzǐ Yóuxiāng：bzdqf@xmrzfpje.biz.cn

Zhe Guo Leng, Yu Zheng Hotel, 362 Po Ji Road, Silla District, Longyan, Fujian. Postal Code: 364452. Phone Number：18017292. E-mail：bzdqf@xmrzfpje.biz.cn

1369。姓名：罗智化

住址（医院）：福建省莆田市秀屿区红学路 936 号世民医院（邮政编码：302719）。联系电话：58440720。电子邮箱：faivo@aygvsemf.health.cn

Zhù zhǐ: Luō Zhì Huà Fújiàn Shěng Pútián Shì Xiù Yǔ Qū Hóng Xué Lù 936 Hào Shì Mín Yī Yuàn (Yóuzhèng Biānmǎ：302719). Liánxì Diànhuà：58440720. Diànzǐ Yóuxiāng：faivo@aygvsemf.health.cn

Zhi Hua Luo, Shi Min Hospital, 936 Hong Xue Road, Xiuyu District, Putian, Fujian. Postal Code: 302719. Phone Number：58440720. E-mail：faivo@aygvsemf.health.cn

1370。姓名：臧近黎

住址（家庭）：福建省厦门市同安区发咚路 209 号焯宽公寓 11 层 360 室
（邮政编码：534940）。联系电话：45707673。电子邮箱：
iscnj@wugfrcad.cn

Zhù zhǐ: Zāng Jìn Lí Fújiàn Shěng Xiàmén Shì Tóngān Qū Fā Dōng Lù 209 Hào Zhuō
Kuān Gōng Yù 11 Céng 360 Shì (Yóuzhèng Biānmǎ：534940). Liánxì Diànhuà：
45707673. Diànzǐ Yóuxiāng：iscnj@wugfrcad.cn

Jin Li Zang, Room# 360, Floor# 11, Zhuo Kuan Apartment, 209 Fa Dong Road,
Tongan District, Xiamen, Fujian. Postal Code: 534940. Phone Number：45707673.
E-mail：iscnj@wugfrcad.cn

1371。姓名：侯寰风

住址（酒店）：福建省莆田市涵江区谢铁路 788 号尚亚酒店（邮政编码：
953452）。联系电话：20328744。电子邮箱：yhlxw@vwbnjdks.biz.cn

Zhù zhǐ: Hóu Huán Fēng Fújiàn Shěng Pútián Shì Hánjiāng Qū Xiè Tiě Lù 788 Hào
Shàng Yà Jiǔ Diàn (Yóuzhèng Biānmǎ：953452). Liánxì Diànhuà：20328744.
Diànzǐ Yóuxiāng：yhlxw@vwbnjdks.biz.cn

Huan Feng Hou, Shang Ya Hotel, 788 Xie Tie Road, Hanjiang District, Putian, Fujian.
Postal Code: 953452. Phone Number：20328744. E-mail：
yhlxw@vwbnjdks.biz.cn

1372。姓名：益大金

住址（寺庙）：福建省宁德市福安市立近路 387 号进葛寺（邮政编码：
453435）。联系电话：43176796。电子邮箱：wklhf@pvsltkxe.god.cn

Zhù zhǐ: Yì Dà Jīn Fújiàn Shěng Níngdé Shì Fúān Shì Lì Jìn Lù 387 Hào Jìn Gé Sì
(Yóuzhèng Biānmǎ：453435). Liánxì Diànhuà：43176796. Diànzǐ Yóuxiāng：
wklhf@pvsltkxe.god.cn

Da Jin Yi, Jin Ge Temple, 387 Li Jin Road, Fuan, Ningde, Fujian. Postal Code: 453435. Phone Number：43176796. E-mail：wklhf@pvsltkxe.god.cn

1373。姓名: 危近九

住址（公共汽车站）：福建省南平市建阳区冕珂路 765 号计钢站（邮政编码：550423）。联系电话：99516916。电子邮箱：uklip@yabupdos.transport.cn

Zhù zhǐ: Wēi Jìn Jiǔ Fújiàn Shěng Nánpíng Shì Jiàn Yáng Qū Miǎn Kē Lù 765 Hào Jì Gāng Zhàn（Yóuzhèng Biānmǎ：550423). Liánxì Diànhuà：99516916. Diànzǐ Yóuxiāng：uklip@yabupdos.transport.cn

Jin Jiu Wei, Ji Gang Bus Station, 765 Mian Ke Road, Jianyang District, Nanping, Fujian. Postal Code: 550423. Phone Number：99516916. E-mail：uklip@yabupdos.transport.cn

1374。姓名: 谭奎澜

住址（博物院）：福建省龙岩市连城县近汉路 969 号龙岩博物馆（邮政编码：175480）。联系电话：49094927。电子邮箱：cprwd@shulxzvb.museums.cn

Zhù zhǐ: Tán Kuí Lán Fújiàn Shěng Lóngyán Shì Liánchéng Xiàn Jìn Hàn Lù 969 Hào Lóngyán Bó Wù Guǎn（Yóuzhèng Biānmǎ：175480). Liánxì Diànhuà：49094927. Diànzǐ Yóuxiāng：cprwd@shulxzvb.museums.cn

Kui Lan Tan, Longyan Museum, 969 Jin Han Road, Liancheng County, Longyan, Fujian. Postal Code: 175480. Phone Number：49094927. E-mail：cprwd@shulxzvb.museums.cn

1375。姓名: 万焯泽

住址（酒店）：福建省莆田市涵江区威铭路 493 号焯德酒店（邮政编码：692430）。联系电话：91866495。电子邮箱：dfwpc@khjmolur.biz.cn

Zhù zhǐ: Wàn Chāo Zé Fújiàn Shěng Pútián Shì Hánjiāng Qū Wēi Míng Lù 493 Hào Chāo Dé Jiǔ Diàn (Yóuzhèng Biānmǎ：692430). Liánxì Diànhuà：91866495. Diànzǐ Yóuxiāng：dfwpc@khjmolur.biz.cn

Chao Ze Wan, Chao De Hotel, 493 Wei Ming Road, Hanjiang District, Putian, Fujian. Postal Code: 692430. Phone Number：91866495. E-mail：dfwpc@khjmolur.biz.cn

1376。姓名: 别金惟

住址（博物院）：福建省福州市台江区俊领路 503 号福州博物馆（邮政编码：682624）。联系电话：59652343。电子邮箱：ntjfb@sdriayvj.museums.cn

Zhù zhǐ: Bié Jīn Wéi Fújiàn Shěng Fúzhōu Shì Tái Jiāng Qū Jùn Lǐng Lù 503 Hào Fúzōu Bó Wù Guǎn (Yóuzhèng Biānmǎ：682624). Liánxì Diànhuà：59652343. Diànzǐ Yóuxiāng：ntjfb@sdriayvj.museums.cn

Jin Wei Bie, Fuzhou Museum, 503 Jun Ling Road, Taijiang District, Fuzhou, Fujian. Postal Code: 682624. Phone Number：59652343. E-mail：ntjfb@sdriayvj.museums.cn

1377。姓名: 单辉科

住址（火车站）：福建省南平市政和县涛冠路 535 号南平站（邮政编码：408789）。联系电话：14975899。电子邮箱：wfyel@ovhimkpy.chr.cn

Zhù zhǐ: Shàn Huī Kē Fújiàn Shěng Nánpíng Shì Zhènghé Xiàn Tāo Guān Lù 535 Hào Nánpíng Zhàn (Yóuzhèng Biānmǎ：408789). Liánxì Diànhuà：14975899. Diànzǐ Yóuxiāng：wfyel@ovhimkpy.chr.cn

Hui Ke Shan, Nanping Railway Station, 535 Tao Guan Road, Zhenghe County, Nanping, Fujian. Postal Code: 408789. Phone Number：14975899. E-mail：wfyel@ovhimkpy.chr.cn

1378。姓名: 闵辙全

住址（家庭）：福建省龙岩市漳平市原昌路 686 号食楚公寓 44 层 899 室（邮政编码：465753）。联系电话：61035622。电子邮箱：jrxkv@cygktbfa.cn

Zhù zhǐ: Mǐn Zhé Quán Fújiàn Shěng Lóngyán Shì Zhāng Píngshì Yuán Chāng Lù 686 Hào Sì Chǔ Gōng Yù 44 Céng 899 Shì (Yóuzhèng Biānmǎ：465753). Liánxì Diànhuà：61035622. Diànzǐ Yóuxiāng：jrxkv@cygktbfa.cn

Zhe Quan Min, Room# 899, Floor# 44, Si Chu Apartment, 686 Yuan Chang Road, Zhangping, Longyan, Fujian. Postal Code: 465753. Phone Number：61035622. E-mail：jrxkv@cygktbfa.cn

1379。姓名：曹尚隆

住址（博物院）：福建省平潭综合实验区平潭县咚员路 488 号平潭综合实验区博物馆（邮政编码：666811）。联系电话：62731110。电子邮箱：xzopd@grjetial.museums.cn

Zhù zhǐ: Cáo Shàng Lóng Fújiàn Shěng Píng Tán Zònghé Shíyàn Qū Píng Tán Xiàn Dōng Yún Lù 488 Hào Píng Tán Zòngé íyàn Qū Bó Wù Guǎn (Yóuzhèng Biānmǎ：666811). Liánxì Diànhuà：62731110. Diànzǐ Yóuxiāng：xzopd@grjetial.museums.cn

Shang Long Cao, Pingtan Comprehensive Experimental Area Museum, 488 Dong Yun Road, Pingtan County, Pingtan Comprehensive Experimental Area, Fujian. Postal Code: 666811. Phone Number：62731110. E-mail：xzopd@grjetial.museums.cn

1380。姓名：虞陆熔

住址（酒店）：福建省平潭综合实验区平潭县迅桥路 864 号成国酒店（邮政编码：280542）。联系电话：57548271。电子邮箱：aumsw@gmtparez.biz.cn

Zhù zhǐ: Yú Liù Róng Fújiàn Shěng Píng Tán Zònghé Shíyàn Qū Píng Tán Xiàn Xùn Qiáo Lù 864 Hào Chéng Guó Jiǔ Diàn (Yóuzhèng Biānmǎ：280542). Liánxì Diànhuà：57548271. Diànzǐ Yóuxiāng：aumsw@gmtparez.biz.cn

Liu Rong Yu, Cheng Guo Hotel, 864 Xun Qiao Road, Pingtan County, Pingtan Comprehensive Experimental Area, Fujian. Postal Code: 280542. Phone Number：57548271. E-mail：aumsw@gmtparez.biz.cn

CHAPTER 2: NAME, SURNAME & ADDRESSES (31-60)

1381。姓名: 左郁振

住址（博物院）： 福建省厦门市集美区葆锡路 925 号厦门博物馆（邮政编码：148272）。联系电话：72506539。电子邮箱：gbiot@pfxwribv.museums.cn

Zhù zhǐ: Zuǒ Yù Zhèn Fújiàn Shěng Xiàmén Shì Jíměi Qū Bǎo Xī Lù 925 Hào Xiàmén Bó Wù Guǎn (Yóuzhèng Biānmǎ：148272). Liánxì Diànhuà：72506539. Diànzǐ Yóuxiāng：gbiot@pfxwribv.museums.cn

Yu Zhen Zuo, Xiamen Museum, 925 Bao Xi Road, Jimei District, Xiamen, Fujian. Postal Code: 148272. Phone Number：72506539. E-mail：gbiot@pfxwribv.museums.cn

1382。姓名: 伍国水

住址（医院）： 福建省漳州市芗城区食钦路 954 号懂渊医院（邮政编码：897062）。联系电话：80730639。电子邮箱：ndqkh@fpondzkw.health.cn

Zhù zhǐ: Wǔ Guó Shuǐ Fújiàn Shěng Zhāngzhōu Shì Xiāng Chéngqū Yì Qīn Lù 954 Hào Dǒng Yuān Yī Yuàn (Yóuzhèng Biānmǎ：897062). Liánxì Diànhuà：80730639. Diànzǐ Yóuxiāng：ndqkh@fpondzkw.health.cn

Guo Shui Wu, Dong Yuan Hospital, 954 Yi Qin Road, Xiangcheng District, Zhangzhou, Fujian. Postal Code: 897062. Phone Number：80730639. E-mail：ndqkh@fpondzkw.health.cn

1383。姓名: 曹德辙

住址（公共汽车站）： 福建省龙岩市武平县智威路 759 号阳中站（邮政编码：881998）。联系电话：19920819。电子邮箱：gbxpo@tkapixro.transport.cn

Zhù zhǐ: Cáo Dé Zhé Fújiàn Shěng Lóngyán Shì Wǔpíng Xiàn Zhì Wēi Lù 759 Hào Yáng Zhōng Zhàn (Yóuzhèng Biānmǎ：881998). Liánxì Diànhuà：19920819. Diànzǐ Yóuxiāng：gbxpo@tkapixro.transport.cn

De Zhe Cao, Yang Zhong Bus Station, 759 Zhi Wei Road, Wuping County, Longyan, Fujian. Postal Code: 881998. Phone Number：19920819. E-mail：gbxpo@tkapixro.transport.cn

1384。姓名: 尚辙成

住址（湖泊）：福建省厦门市湖里区盛懂路 239 号队智湖（邮政编码：495965）。联系电话：35750354。电子邮箱：hcwzu@cgdxihwo.lakes.cn

Zhù zhǐ: Shàng Zhé Chéng Fújiàn Shěng Xiàmén Shì Hú Lǐ Qū Shèng Dǒng Lù 239 Hào Duì Zhì Hú (Yóuzhèng Biānmǎ：495965). Liánxì Diànhuà：35750354. Diànzǐ Yóuxiāng：hcwzu@cgdxihwo.lakes.cn

Zhe Cheng Shang, Dui Zhi Lake, 239 Sheng Dong Road, Huli District, Xiamen, Fujian. Postal Code: 495965. Phone Number：35750354. E-mail：hcwzu@cgdxihwo.lakes.cn

1385。姓名: 齐仓珂

住址（寺庙）：福建省龙岩市新罗区熔己路 156 号寰祥寺（邮政编码：624396）。联系电话：42720718。电子邮箱：hjqkm@icejgxuv.god.cn

Zhù zhǐ: Qí Cāng Kē Fújiàn Shěng Lóngyán Shì Xīn Luō Qū Róng Jǐ Lù 156 Hào Huán Xiáng Sì (Yóuzhèng Biānmǎ：624396). Liánxì Diànhuà：42720718. Diànzǐ Yóuxiāng：hjqkm@icejgxuv.god.cn

Cang Ke Qi, Huan Xiang Temple, 156 Rong Ji Road, Silla District, Longyan, Fujian. Postal Code: 624396. Phone Number：42720718. E-mail：hjqkm@icejgxuv.god.cn

1386。姓名: 应阳游

住址（家庭）：福建省三明市永安市成守路 421 号坤可公寓 49 层 323 室（邮政编码：294144）。联系电话：28489946。电子邮箱：hdwqg@pergqhvk.cn

Zhù zhǐ: Yīng Yáng Yóu Fújiàn Shěng Sānmíng Shì Yǒngān Shì Chéng Shǒu Lù 421 Hào Kūn Kě Gōng Yù 49 Céng 323 Shì (Yóuzhèng Biānmǎ：294144). Liánxì Diànhuà：28489946. Diànzǐ Yóuxiāng：hdwqg@pergqhvk.cn

Yang You Ying, Room# 323, Floor# 49, Kun Ke Apartment, 421 Cheng Shou Road, Yongan City, Sanming, Fujian. Postal Code: 294144. Phone Number：28489946. E-mail：hdwqg@pergqhvk.cn

1387。姓名: 夔亭甫

住址（家庭）：福建省泉州市丰泽区兵智路 556 号龙跃公寓 43 层 913 室（邮政编码：500546）。联系电话：69141680。电子邮箱：lwkce@fjrhecdz.cn

Zhù zhǐ: Kuí Tíng Fǔ Fújiàn Shěng Quánzhōu Shì Fēng Zé Qū Bīng Zhì Lù 556 Hào Lóng Yuè Gōng Yù 43 Céng 913 Shì (Yóuzhèng Biānmǎ：500546). Liánxì Diànhuà：69141680. Diànzǐ Yóuxiāng：lwkce@fjrhecdz.cn

Ting Fu Kui, Room# 913, Floor# 43, Long Yue Apartment, 556 Bing Zhi Road, Fengze District, Quanzhou, Fujian. Postal Code: 500546. Phone Number：69141680. E-mail：lwkce@fjrhecdz.cn

1388。姓名: 叶辉昌

住址（大学）：福建省泉州市鲤城区锡游大学俊食路 938 号（邮政编码：390148）。联系电话：97858980。电子邮箱：phmnl@vmhpfyzt.edu.cn

Zhù zhǐ: Yè Huī Chāng Fújiàn Shěng Quánzhōu Shì Lǐ Chéngqū Xī Yóu DàxuéJùn Sì Lù 938 Hào (Yóuzhèng Biānmǎ：390148). Liánxì Diànhuà：97858980. Diànzǐ Yóuxiāng：phmnl@vmhpfyzt.edu.cn

Hui Chang Ye, Xi You University, 938 Jun Si Road, Licheng District, Quanzhou, Fujian. Postal Code: 390148. Phone Number：97858980. E-mail：phmnl@vmhpfyzt.edu.cn

1389。姓名: 呼延学石

住址（公共汽车站）：福建省泉州市晋江市恩庆路 207 号翰毅站（邮政编码：295889）。联系电话：36119531。电子邮箱：rwcqg@xhwzmigy.transport.cn

Zhù zhǐ: Hūyán Xué Shí Fújiàn Shěng Quánzhōu Shì Jìnjiāng Shì Ēn Qìng Lù 207 Hào Hàn Yì Zhàn（Yóuzhèng Biānmǎ：295889). Liánxì Diànhuà：36119531. Diànzǐ Yóuxiāng：rwcqg@xhwzmigy.transport.cn

Xue Shi Huyan, Han Yi Bus Station, 207 En Qing Road, Jinjiang City, Quanzhou, Fujian. Postal Code: 295889. Phone Number：36119531. E-mail：rwcqg@xhwzmigy.transport.cn

1390。姓名：骆大郁

住址（公司）：福建省福州市长乐区兆其路 894 号沛自有限公司（邮政编码：746248）。联系电话：86589207。电子邮箱：qrait@avxfwecl.biz.cn

Zhù zhǐ: Luò Dà Yù Fújiàn Shěng Fúzhōu Shì Zhǎnglè Qū Zhào Qí Lù 894 Hào Pèi Zì Yǒuxiàn Gōngsī（Yóuzhèng Biānmǎ：746248). Liánxì Diànhuà：86589207. Diànzǐ Yóuxiāng：qrait@avxfwecl.biz.cn

Da Yu Luo, Pei Zi Corporation, 894 Zhao Qi Road, Changle District, Fuzhou, Fujian. Postal Code: 746248. Phone Number：86589207. E-mail：qrait@avxfwecl.biz.cn

1391。姓名：左丘亚强

住址（广场）：福建省宁德市柘荣县土亮路 919 号铁跃广场（邮政编码：331641）。联系电话：52917023。电子邮箱：paefl@ujrqnysw.squares.cn

Zhù zhǐ: Zuǒqiū Yà Qiáng Fújiàn Shěng Níngdé Shì Zhè Róngxiàn Tǔ Liàng Lù 919 Hào Fū Yuè Guǎng Chǎng（Yóuzhèng Biānmǎ：331641). Liánxì Diànhuà：52917023. Diànzǐ Yóuxiāng：paefl@ujrqnysw.squares.cn

Ya Qiang Zuoqiu, Fu Yue Square, 919 Tu Liang Road, Zherong County, Ningde, Fujian. Postal Code: 331641. Phone Number：52917023. E-mail：paefl@ujrqnysw.squares.cn

1392。姓名: 诸仓钢

住址（酒店）：福建省龙岩市上杭县谢化路 780 号中民酒店（邮政编码：847546）。联系电话：95081667。电子邮箱：wyilo@qrvjnoig.biz.cn

Zhù zhǐ: Zhū Cāng Gāng Fújiàn Shěng Lóngyán Shì Shàng Háng Xiàn Xiè Huà Lù 780 Hào Zhòng Mín Jiǔ Diàn（Yóuzhèng Biānmǎ：847546). Liánxì Diànhuà：95081667. Diànzǐ Yóuxiāng：wyilo@qrvjnoig.biz.cn

Cang Gang Zhu, Zhong Min Hotel, 780 Xie Hua Road, Shanghang County, Longyan, Fujian. Postal Code: 847546. Phone Number：95081667. E-mail：wyilo@qrvjnoig.biz.cn

1393。姓名: 范员九

住址（医院）：福建省三明市建宁县黎黎路 984 号际际医院（邮政编码：687262）。联系电话：57967785。电子邮箱：ovmfl@hrwksmoj.health.cn

Zhù zhǐ: Fàn Yún Jiǔ Fújiàn Shěng Sānmíng Shì Jiàn Níngxiàn Lí Lí Lù 984 Hào Jì Jì Yī Yuàn（Yóuzhèng Biānmǎ：687262). Liánxì Diànhuà：57967785. Diànzǐ Yóuxiāng：ovmfl@hrwksmoj.health.cn

Yun Jiu Fan, Ji Ji Hospital, 984 Li Li Road, Jianning County, Sanming, Fujian. Postal Code: 687262. Phone Number：57967785. E-mail：ovmfl@hrwksmoj.health.cn

1394。姓名: 刁斌德

住址（大学）：福建省福州市仓山区浩愈大学科坤路 789 号（邮政编码：340872）。联系电话：48566810。电子邮箱：mhavx@laumytvd.edu.cn

Zhù zhǐ: Diāo Bīn Dé Fújiàn Shěng Fúzhōu Shì Cāng Shānqū Hào Yù DàxuéKē Kūn Lù 789 Hào（Yóuzhèng Biānmǎ：340872). Liánxì Diànhuà：48566810. Diànzǐ Yóuxiāng：mhavx@laumytvd.edu.cn

Bin De Diao, Hao Yu University, 789 Ke Kun Road, Cangshan District, Fuzhou, Fujian. Postal Code: 340872. Phone Number：48566810. E-mail：mhavx@laumytvd.edu.cn

1395。姓名: 索秀跃

住址（公共汽车站）：福建省莆田市仙游县辙石路 950 号郁陆站（邮政编码：766499）。联系电话：14066251。电子邮箱：axejp@satkzgud.transport.cn

Zhù zhǐ: Suǒ Xiù Yuè Fújiàn Shěng Pútián Shì Xiān Yóu Xiàn Zhé Dàn Lù 950 Hào Yù Liù Zhàn (Yóuzhèng Biānmǎ：766499). Liánxì Diànhuà：14066251. Diànzǐ Yóuxiāng：axejp@satkzgud.transport.cn

Xiu Yue Suo, Yu Liu Bus Station, 950 Zhe Dan Road, Xianyou County, Putian, Fujian. Postal Code: 766499. Phone Number：14066251. E-mail：axejp@satkzgud.transport.cn

1396。姓名: 逢翼仓

住址（医院）：福建省漳州市龙海区仓宝路 431 号盛锤医院（邮政编码：594183）。联系电话：88233099。电子邮箱：jcwqa@tkedqxpa.health.cn

Zhù zhǐ: Páng Yì Cāng Fújiàn Shěng Zhāngzhōu Shì Lóng Hǎiqū Cāng Bǎo Lù 431 Hào Shèng Chuí Yī Yuàn (Yóuzhèng Biānmǎ：594183). Liánxì Diànhuà：88233099. Diànzǐ Yóuxiāng：jcwqa@tkedqxpa.health.cn

Yi Cang Pang, Sheng Chui Hospital, 431 Cang Bao Road, Longhai District, Zhangzhou, Fujian. Postal Code: 594183. Phone Number：88233099. E-mail：jcwqa@tkedqxpa.health.cn

1397。姓名: 支毅员

住址（机场）：福建省南平市松溪县龙翰路 211 号南平风亮国际机场（邮政编码：966626）。联系电话：31644720。电子邮箱：pfrzx@tslhgvqu.airports.cn

Zhù zhǐ: Zhī Yì Yuán Fújiàn Shěng Nánpíng Shì Sōng Xī Xiàn Lóng Hàn Lù 211 Hào Nánpíng Fēng Liàng Guó Jì Jī Chǎng（Yóuzhèng Biānmǎ：966626）. Liánxì Diànhuà：31644720. Diànzǐ Yóuxiāng：pfrzx@tslhgvqu.airports.cn

Yi Yuan Zhi, Nanping Feng Liang International Airport, 211 Long Han Road, Songxi County, Nanping, Fujian. Postal Code: 966626. Phone Number：31644720. E-mail：pfrzx@tslhgvqu.airports.cn

1398。姓名: 岳员铁

住址（酒店）：福建省南平市松溪县不盛路 176 号岐迅酒店（邮政编码：582482）。联系电话：19192641。电子邮箱：hgfte@bwafcqzo.biz.cn

Zhù zhǐ: Yuè Yuán Tiě Fújiàn Shěng Nánpíng Shì Sōng Xī Xiàn Bù Chéng Lù 176 Hào Qí Xùn Jiǔ Diàn（Yóuzhèng Biānmǎ：582482）. Liánxì Diànhuà：19192641. Diànzǐ Yóuxiāng：hgfte@bwafcqzo.biz.cn

Yuan Tie Yue, Qi Xun Hotel, 176 Bu Cheng Road, Songxi County, Nanping, Fujian. Postal Code: 582482. Phone Number：19192641. E-mail：hgfte@bwafcqzo.biz.cn

1399。姓名: 隆渊来

住址（寺庙）：福建省三明市大田县坚腾路 265 号铁亮寺（邮政编码：779138）。联系电话：20729805。电子邮箱：lmbis@bltgshmu.god.cn

Zhù zhǐ: Lóng Yuān Lái Fújiàn Shěng Sānmíng Shì Dàtián Xiàn Jiān Téng Lù 265 Hào Tiě Liàng Sì（Yóuzhèng Biānmǎ：779138）. Liánxì Diànhuà：20729805. Diànzǐ Yóuxiāng：lmbis@bltgshmu.god.cn

Yuan Lai Long, Tie Liang Temple, 265 Jian Teng Road, Datian County, Sanming, Fujian. Postal Code: 779138. Phone Number：20729805. E-mail：lmbis@bltgshmu.god.cn

1400。姓名: 单胜禹

住址（大学）：福建省泉州市惠安县来自大学跃强路 155 号（邮政编码：681892）。联系电话：12842991。电子邮箱：nmxlg@sajlqpzr.edu.cn

Zhù zhǐ: Shàn Shēng Yǔ Fújiàn Shěng Quánzhōu Shì Huìānxiàn Lái Zì DàxuéYuè Qiǎng Lù 155 Hào（Yóuzhèng Biānmǎ：681892). Liánxì Diànhuà：12842991. Diànzǐ Yóuxiāng：nmxlg@sajlqpzr.edu.cn

Sheng Yu Shan, Lai Zi University, 155 Yue Qiang Road, Huian County, Quanzhou, Fujian. Postal Code: 681892. Phone Number：12842991. E-mail：nmxlg@sajlqpzr.edu.cn

1401。姓名: 褚磊可

住址（机场）：福建省南平市政和县炯克路 291 号南平征食国际机场（邮政编码：757180）。联系电话：96300309。电子邮箱：ikuzn@gwezbaqt.airports.cn

Zhù zhǐ: Chǔ Lěi Kě Fújiàn Shěng Nánpíng Shì Zhènghé Xiàn Jiǒng Kè Lù 291 Hào Nánpíng Zhēng Yì Guó Jì Jī Chǎng（Yóuzhèng Biānmǎ：757180). Liánxì Diànhuà：96300309. Diànzǐ Yóuxiāng：ikuzn@gwezbaqt.airports.cn

Lei Ke Chu, Nanping Zheng Yi International Airport, 291 Jiong Ke Road, Zhenghe County, Nanping, Fujian. Postal Code: 757180. Phone Number：96300309. E-mail：ikuzn@gwezbaqt.airports.cn

1402。姓名: 咸迅翼

住址（公共汽车站）：福建省南平市武夷山市磊谢路 475 号骥屹站（邮政编码：757084）。联系电话：38438738。电子邮箱：mafie@ajwfmbpi.transport.cn

Zhù zhǐ: Xián Xùn Yì Fújiàn Shěng Nánpíng Shì Wǔyíshān Shì Lěi Xiè Lù 475 Hào Jì Yì Zhàn（Yóuzhèng Biānmǎ：757084). Liánxì Diànhuà：38438738. Diànzǐ Yóuxiāng：mafie@ajwfmbpi.transport.cn

Xun Yi Xian, Ji Yi Bus Station, 475 Lei Xie Road, Wuyishan City, Nanping, Fujian. Postal Code: 757084. Phone Number：38438738. E-mail：mafie@ajwfmbpi.transport.cn

1403。姓名: 葛其队

住址（公司）：福建省泉州市石狮市葛楚路 434 号己豹有限公司（邮政编码：933279）。联系电话：80120299。电子邮箱：xpeys@mblhnjvw.biz.cn

Zhù zhǐ: Gě Qí Duì Fújiàn Shěng Quánzhōu Shì Shíshī Shì Gé Chǔ Lù 434 Hào Jǐ Bào Yǒuxiàn Gōngsī (Yóuzhèng Biānmǎ：933279). Liánxì Diànhuà：80120299. Diànzǐ Yóuxiāng：xpeys@mblhnjvw.biz.cn

Qi Dui Ge, Ji Bao Corporation, 434 Ge Chu Road, Shishi, Quanzhou, Fujian. Postal Code: 933279. Phone Number：80120299. E-mail：xpeys@mblhnjvw.biz.cn

1404。姓名: 齐乙俊

住址（家庭）：福建省龙岩市上杭县恩易路 304 号科成公寓 36 层 542 室（邮政编码：141416）。联系电话：43476182。电子邮箱：xmsfd@yskgnjle.cn

Zhù zhǐ: Qí Yǐ Jùn Fújiàn Shěng Lóngyán Shì Shàng Háng Xiàn Ēn Yì Lù 304 Hào Kē Chéng Gōng Yù 36 Céng 542 Shì (Yóuzhèng Biānmǎ：141416). Liánxì Diànhuà：43476182. Diànzǐ Yóuxiāng：xmsfd@yskgnjle.cn

Yi Jun Qi, Room# 542, Floor# 36, Ke Cheng Apartment, 304 En Yi Road, Shanghang County, Longyan, Fujian. Postal Code: 141416. Phone Number：43476182. E-mail：xmsfd@yskgnjle.cn

1405。姓名: 乔兆轶

住址（公司）：福建省宁德市屏南县顺食路 289 号楚锡有限公司（邮政编码：257809）。联系电话：19685311。电子邮箱：hdbfg@oxlwirsn.biz.cn

Zhù zhǐ: Qiáo Zhào Yì Fújiàn Shěng Níngdé Shì Píng Nán Xiàn Shùn Sì Lù 289 Hào Chǔ Xī Yǒuxiàn Gōngsī (Yóuzhèng Biānmǎ: 257809). Liánxì Diànhuà: 19685311. Diànzǐ Yóuxiāng: hdbfg@oxlwirsn.biz.cn

Zhao Yi Qiao, Chu Xi Corporation, 289 Shun Si Road, Pingnan County, Ningde, Fujian. Postal Code: 257809. Phone Number: 19685311. E-mail: hdbfg@oxlwirsn.biz.cn

1406。姓名: 靳强盛

住址（公司）：福建省宁德市屏南县庆九路 424 号振陆有限公司（邮政编码：859763）。联系电话：80052333。电子邮箱：stgkc@rtfpcaew.biz.cn

Zhù zhǐ: Jìn Qiǎng Shèng Fújiàn Shěng Níngdé Shì Píng Nán Xiàn Qìng Jiǔ Lù 424 Hào Zhèn Lù Yǒuxiàn Gōngsī (Yóuzhèng Biānmǎ: 859763). Liánxì Diànhuà: 80052333. Diànzǐ Yóuxiāng: stgkc@rtfpcaew.biz.cn

Qiang Sheng Jin, Zhen Lu Corporation, 424 Qing Jiu Road, Pingnan County, Ningde, Fujian. Postal Code: 859763. Phone Number: 80052333. E-mail: stgkc@rtfpcaew.biz.cn

1407。姓名: 管舟亭

住址（大学）：福建省三明市清流县乐轼大学斌学路 867 号（邮政编码：332132）。联系电话：30022383。电子邮箱：rgnqe@fuirbvcm.edu.cn

Zhù zhǐ: Guǎn Zhōu Tíng Fújiàn Shěng Sānmíng Shì Qīngliú Xiàn Lè Shì Dàxué Bīn Xué Lù 867 Hào (Yóuzhèng Biānmǎ: 332132). Liánxì Diànhuà: 30022383. Diànzǐ Yóuxiāng: rgnqe@fuirbvcm.edu.cn

Zhou Ting Guan, Le Shi University, 867 Bin Xue Road, Qingliu County, Sanming, Fujian. Postal Code: 332132. Phone Number: 30022383. E-mail: rgnqe@fuirbvcm.edu.cn

1408。姓名: 有乐科

住址（大学）：福建省三明市大田县冠进大学翰强路 928 号（邮政编码：386369）。联系电话：60273915。电子邮箱：iwgoc@cfvksjzw.edu.cn

Zhù zhǐ: Yǒu Lè Kē Fújiàn Shěng Sānmíng Shì Dàtián Xiàn Guān Jìn DàxuéHàn Qiǎng Lù 928 Hào（Yóuzhèng Biānmǎ：386369). Liánxì Diànhuà：60273915. Diànzǐ Yóuxiāng：iwgoc@cfvksjzw.edu.cn

Le Ke You, Guan Jin University, 928 Han Qiang Road, Datian County, Sanming, Fujian. Postal Code: 386369. Phone Number：60273915. E-mail：iwgoc@cfvksjzw.edu.cn

1409。姓名: 乜盛屹

住址（寺庙）：福建省泉州市德化县石沛路 392 号黎冠寺（邮政编码：969056）。联系电话：62446465。电子邮箱：zkgfr@fbpzdqvl.god.cn

Zhù zhǐ: Niè Chéng Yì Fújiàn Shěng Quánzhōu Shì Dé Huà Xiàn Dàn Bèi Lù 392 Hào Lí Guān Sì（Yóuzhèng Biānmǎ：969056). Liánxì Diànhuà：62446465. Diànzǐ Yóuxiāng：zkgfr@fbpzdqvl.god.cn

Cheng Yi Nie, Li Guan Temple, 392 Dan Bei Road, Dehua County, Quanzhou, Fujian. Postal Code: 969056. Phone Number：62446465. E-mail：zkgfr@fbpzdqvl.god.cn

1410。姓名: 晋宽守

住址（火车站）：福建省福州市仓山区队柱路 201 号福州站（邮政编码：444698）。联系电话：32839928。电子邮箱：jhogr@xqcrazkl.chr.cn

Zhù zhǐ: Jìn Kuān Shǒu Fújiàn Shěng Fúzhōu Shì Cāng Shānqū Duì Zhù Lù 201 Hào Fúzōu Zhàn（Yóuzhèng Biānmǎ：444698). Liánxì Diànhuà：32839928. Diànzǐ Yóuxiāng：jhogr@xqcrazkl.chr.cn

Kuan Shou Jin, Fuzhou Railway Station, 201 Dui Zhu Road, Cangshan District, Fuzhou, Fujian. Postal Code: 444698. Phone Number：32839928. E-mail：jhogr@xqcrazkl.chr.cn

CHAPTER 3: NAME, SURNAME & ADDRESSES (61-90)

1411。姓名: 阳星禹

住址（博物院）：福建省三明市尤溪县锤乙路 753 号三明博物馆（邮政编码：586874）。联系电话：74184012。电子邮箱：ernsp@itwexfuo.museums.cn

Zhù zhǐ: Yáng Xīng Yǔ Fújiàn Shěng Sānmíng Shì Yóu Xī Xiàn Chuí Yǐ Lù 753 Hào ānmíng Bó Wù Guǎn (Yóuzhèng Biānmǎ：586874). Liánxì Diànhuà：74184012. Diànzǐ Yóuxiāng：ernsp@itwexfuo.museums.cn

Xing Yu Yang, Sanming Museum, 753 Chui Yi Road, Youxi County, Sanming, Fujian. Postal Code: 586874. Phone Number：74184012. E-mail：ernsp@itwexfuo.museums.cn

1412。姓名: 屠甫圣

住址（湖泊）：福建省福州市永泰县波土路 693 号钊陆湖（邮政编码：918398）。联系电话：27755221。电子邮箱：ahfjm@ypbfnteo.lakes.cn

Zhù zhǐ: Tú Fǔ Shèng Fújiàn Shěng Fúzhōu Shì Yǒngtài Xiàn Bō Tǔ Lù 693 Hào Zhāo Lù Hú (Yóuzhèng Biānmǎ：918398). Liánxì Diànhuà：27755221. Diànzǐ Yóuxiāng：ahfjm@ypbfnteo.lakes.cn

Fu Sheng Tu, Zhao Lu Lake, 693 Bo Tu Road, Yongtai County, Fuzhou, Fujian. Postal Code: 918398. Phone Number：27755221. E-mail：ahfjm@ypbfnteo.lakes.cn

1413。姓名: 南门源波

住址（大学）：福建省漳州市长泰区员不大学洵山路 956 号（邮政编码：199231）。联系电话：56040228。电子邮箱：jpawi@nxwojzau.edu.cn

Zhù zhǐ: Nánmén Yuán Bō Fújiàn Shěng Zhāngzhōu Shì Zhǎng Tài Qū Yún Bù DàxuéXún Shān Lù 956 Hào (Yóuzhèng Biānmǎ：199231). Liánxì Diànhuà：56040228. Diànzǐ Yóuxiāng：jpawi@nxwojzau.edu.cn

Yuan Bo Nanmen, Yun Bu University, 956 Xun Shan Road, Changtai District, Zhangzhou, Fujian. Postal Code: 199231. Phone Number：56040228. E-mail：jpawi@nxwojzau.edu.cn

1414。姓名: 樊民民

住址（医院）：福建省宁德市寿宁县洵水路 343 号奎友医院（邮政编码：411556）。联系电话：73840094。电子邮箱：gnwht@gsxrnbyf.health.cn

Zhù zhǐ: Fán Mín Mín Fújiàn Shěng Níngdé Shì Shòu Níngxiàn Xún Shuǐ Lù 343 Hào Kuí Yǒu Yī Yuàn（Yóuzhèng Biānmǎ：411556). Liánxì Diànhuà：73840094. Diànzǐ Yóuxiāng：gnwht@gsxrnbyf.health.cn

Min Min Fan, Kui You Hospital, 343 Xun Shui Road, Shouning County, Ningde, Fujian. Postal Code: 411556. Phone Number：73840094. E-mail：gnwht@gsxrnbyf.health.cn

1415。姓名: 钟柱刚

住址（大学）：福建省福州市晋安区轼其大学守威路 775 号（邮政编码：686833）。联系电话：16014759。电子邮箱：kpghx@teqngwpi.edu.cn

Zhù zhǐ: Zhōng Zhù Gāng Fújiàn Shěng Fúzhōu Shì Jìn Ān Qū Shì Qí DàxuéShǒu Wēi Lù 775 Hào（Yóuzhèng Biānmǎ：686833). Liánxì Diànhuà：16014759. Diànzǐ Yóuxiāng：kpghx@teqngwpi.edu.cn

Zhu Gang Zhong, Shi Qi University, 775 Shou Wei Road, Jinan District, Fuzhou, Fujian. Postal Code: 686833. Phone Number：16014759. E-mail：kpghx@teqngwpi.edu.cn

1416。姓名: 樊陆鹤

住址（公园）：福建省厦门市同安区懂南路 148 号帆勇公园（邮政编码：694306）。联系电话：34539913。电子邮箱：updly@vadbmkft.parks.cn

Zhù zhǐ: Fán Lù Hè Fújiàn Shěng Xiàmén Shì Tóngān Qū Dǒng Nán Lù 148 Hào Fān Yǒng Gōng Yuán (Yóuzhèng Biānmǎ: 694306). Liánxì Diànhuà: 34539913. Diànzǐ Yóuxiāng: updly@vadbmkft.parks.cn

Lu He Fan, Fan Yong Park, 148 Dong Nan Road, Tongan District, Xiamen, Fujian. Postal Code: 694306. Phone Number: 34539913. E-mail: updly@vadbmkft.parks.cn

1417。姓名: 秋大大

住址（公司）：福建省南平市延平区歧宝路 962 号浩焯有限公司（邮政编码：448616）。联系电话：70795020。电子邮箱：tkycv@sjbivfrw.biz.cn

Zhù zhǐ: Qiū Dà Dài Fújiàn Shěng Nánpíng Shì Yánpíng Qū Qí Bǎo Lù 962 Hào Hào Chāo Yǒuxiàn Gōngsī (Yóuzhèng Biānmǎ: 448616). Liánxì Diànhuà: 70795020. Diànzǐ Yóuxiāng: tkycv@sjbivfrw.biz.cn

Da Dai Qiu, Hao Chao Corporation, 962 Qi Bao Road, Yanping District, Nanping, Fujian. Postal Code: 448616. Phone Number: 70795020. E-mail: tkycv@sjbivfrw.biz.cn

1418。姓名: 易涛寰

住址（家庭）：福建省莆田市城厢区世咚路 313 号强兵公寓 18 层 698 室（邮政编码：784132）。联系电话：43706394。电子邮箱：abvjy@hitofsdp.cn

Zhù zhǐ: Yì Tāo Huán Fújiàn Shěng Pútián Shì Chéngxiāng Qū Shì Dōng Lù 313 Hào Qiǎng Bīng Gōng Yù 18 Céng 698 Shì (Yóuzhèng Biānmǎ: 784132). Liánxì Diànhuà: 43706394. Diànzǐ Yóuxiāng: abvjy@hitofsdp.cn

Tao Huan Yi, Room# 698, Floor# 18, Qiang Bing Apartment, 313 Shi Dong Road, Chengxiang District, Putian, Fujian. Postal Code: 784132. Phone Number: 43706394. E-mail: abvjy@hitofsdp.cn

1419。姓名: 丰员仲

住址（大学）：福建省厦门市海沧区威大大学岐辉路 916 号（邮政编码：602265）。联系电话：85219775。电子邮箱：wnevx@fhydzavt.edu.cn

Zhù zhǐ: Fēng Yún Zhòng Fújiàn Shěng Xiàmén Shì Hǎi Cāng Qū Wēi Dà DàxuéQí Huī Lù 916 Hào（Yóuzhèng Biānmǎ：602265). Liánxì Diànhuà：85219775. Diànzǐ Yóuxiāng：wnevx@fhydzavt.edu.cn

Yun Zhong Feng, Wei Da University, 916 Qi Hui Road, Haicang District, Xiamen, Fujian. Postal Code: 602265. Phone Number：85219775. E-mail：wnevx@fhydzavt.edu.cn

1420。姓名: 柴亭大

住址（机场）：福建省宁德市周宁县福炯路 220 号宁德白葆国际机场（邮政编码：161501）。联系电话：54103630。电子邮箱：yzxsi@clvthnfz.airports.cn

Zhù zhǐ: Chái Tíng Dà Fújiàn Shěng Níngdé Shì Zhōu Níngxiàn Fú Jiǒng Lù 220 Hào Níngdé Bái Bǎo Guó Jì Jī Chǎng（Yóuzhèng Biānmǎ：161501). Liánxì Diànhuà：54103630. Diànzǐ Yóuxiāng：yzxsi@clvthnfz.airports.cn

Ting Da Chai, Ningde Bai Bao International Airport, 220 Fu Jiong Road, Zhouning County, Ningde, Fujian. Postal Code: 161501. Phone Number：54103630. E-mail：yzxsi@clvthnfz.airports.cn

1421。姓名: 许星先

住址（机场）：福建省莆田市荔城区领乙路 674 号莆田院珂国际机场（邮政编码：254038）。联系电话：36994275。电子邮箱：latfo@ojumvweh.airports.cn

Zhù zhǐ: Xǔ Xīng Xiān Fújiàn Shěng Pútián Shì Lì Chéngqū Lǐng Yǐ Lù 674 Hào Pútián Yuàn Kē Guó Jì Jī Chǎng（Yóuzhèng Biānmǎ：254038). Liánxì Diànhuà：36994275. Diànzǐ Yóuxiāng：latfo@ojumvweh.airports.cn

Xing Xian Xu, Putian Yuan Ke International Airport, 674 Ling Yi Road, Licheng District, Putian, Fujian. Postal Code: 254038. Phone Number：36994275. E-mail：latfo@ojumvweh.airports.cn

1422。姓名: 边骥郁

住址（医院）: 福建省厦门市翔安区王陆路 689 号跃克医院（邮政编码：293466）。联系电话：61909951。电子邮箱：ecjmy@mqhxpisu.health.cn

Zhù zhǐ: Biān Jì Yù Fújiàn Shěng Xiàmén Shì Xiáng Ān Qū Wàng Liù Lù 689 Hào Yuè Kè Yī Yuàn（Yóuzhèng Biānmǎ：293466). Liánxì Diànhuà：61909951. Diànzǐ Yóuxiāng：ecjmy@mqhxpisu.health.cn

Ji Yu Bian, Yue Ke Hospital, 689 Wang Liu Road, Xiangan District, Xiamen, Fujian. Postal Code: 293466. Phone Number：61909951. E-mail：ecjmy@mqhxpisu.health.cn

1423。姓名: 燕坚中

住址（家庭）: 福建省莆田市秀屿区熔铁路 234 号歧郁公寓 49 层 825 室（邮政编码：816592）。联系电话：72692350。电子邮箱：aplnr@exnkcbws.cn

Zhù zhǐ: Yān Jiān Zhōng Fújiàn Shěng Pútián Shì Xiù Yǔ Qū Róng Tiě Lù 234 Hào Qí Yù Gōng Yù 49 Céng 825 Shì (Yóuzhèng Biānmǎ：816592). Liánxì Diànhuà：72692350. Diànzǐ Yóuxiāng：aplnr@exnkcbws.cn

Jian Zhong Yan, Room# 825, Floor# 49, Qi Yu Apartment, 234 Rong Tie Road, Xiuyu District, Putian, Fujian. Postal Code: 816592. Phone Number：72692350. E-mail：aplnr@exnkcbws.cn

1424。姓名: 仇督陆奎

住址（公园）: 福建省平潭综合实验区平潭县斌全路 514 号敬圣公园（邮政编码：554421）。联系电话：68790886。电子邮箱：dywlf@jdmaerpl.parks.cn

Zhù zhǐ: Zhǎngdū Lù Kuí Fújiàn Shěng Píng Tán Zònghé Shíyàn Qū Píng Tán Xiàn Bīn Quán Lù 514 Hào Jìng Shèng Gōng Yuán（Yóuzhèng Biānmǎ：554421). Liánxì Diànhuà：68790886. Diànzǐ Yóuxiāng：dywlf@jdmaerpl.parks.cn

Lu Kui Zhangdu, Jing Sheng Park, 514 Bin Quan Road, Pingtan County, Pingtan Comprehensive Experimental Area, Fujian. Postal Code: 554421. Phone Number：68790886. E-mail：dywlf@jdmaerpl.parks.cn

1425。姓名: 充中庆

住址（大学）：福建省厦门市湖里区红绅大学葛秀路 260 号（邮政编码：264444）。联系电话：57878259。电子邮箱：guhkr@gcpqzrtk.edu.cn

Zhù zhǐ: Chōng Zhōng Qìng Fújiàn Shěng Xiàmén Shì Hú Lǐ Qū Hóng Shēn DàxuéGé Xiù Lù 260 Hào（Yóuzhèng Biānmǎ：264444). Liánxì Diànhuà：57878259. Diànzǐ Yóuxiāng：guhkr@gcpqzrtk.edu.cn

Zhong Qing Chong, Hong Shen University, 260 Ge Xiu Road, Huli District, Xiamen, Fujian. Postal Code: 264444. Phone Number：57878259. E-mail：guhkr@gcpqzrtk.edu.cn

1426。姓名: 莘焯仲

住址（火车站）：福建省厦门市思明区咚鹤路 207 号厦门站（邮政编码：762830）。联系电话：17650359。电子邮箱：aqhxj@sjbghauf.chr.cn

Zhù zhǐ: Shēn Chāo Zhòng Fújiàn Shěng Xiàmén Shì Sī Míng Qū Dōng Hè Lù 207 Hào Xiàmén Zhàn（Yóuzhèng Biānmǎ：762830). Liánxì Diànhuà：17650359. Diànzǐ Yóuxiāng：aqhxj@sjbghauf.chr.cn

Chao Zhong Shen, Xiamen Railway Station, 207 Dong He Road, Siming District, Xiamen, Fujian. Postal Code: 762830. Phone Number：17650359. E-mail：aqhxj@sjbghauf.chr.cn

1427。姓名: 萧炯盛

住址（公共汽车站）：福建省厦门市翔安区坡坤路 999 号顺全站（邮政编码：239694）。联系电话：16851371。电子邮箱：maxjk@mowxfbdu.transport.cn

Zhù zhǐ: Xiāo Jiǒng Chéng Fújiàn Shěng Xiàmén Shì Xiáng Ān Qū Pō Kūn Lù 999 Hào Shùn Quán Zhàn（Yóuzhèng Biānmǎ：239694). Liánxì Diànhuà：16851371. Diànzǐ Yóuxiāng：maxjk@mowxfbdu.transport.cn

Jiong Cheng Xiao, Shun Quan Bus Station, 999 Po Kun Road, Xiangan District, Xiamen, Fujian. Postal Code: 239694. Phone Number：16851371. E-mail：maxjk@mowxfbdu.transport.cn

1428。姓名: 伊恩学

住址（公园）：福建省宁德市福鼎市继游路 513 号易祥公园（邮政编码：242400）。联系电话：75958022。电子邮箱：cjisq@lxdjzypg.parks.cn

Zhù zhǐ: Yī Ēn Xué Fújiàn Shěng Níngdé Shì Fú Dǐng Shì Jì Yóu Lù 513 Hào Yì Xiáng Gōng Yuán（Yóuzhèng Biānmǎ：242400). Liánxì Diànhuà：75958022. Diànzǐ Yóuxiāng：cjisq@lxdjzypg.parks.cn

En Xue Yi, Yi Xiang Park, 513 Ji You Road, Fuding City, Ningde, Fujian. Postal Code: 242400. Phone Number：75958022. E-mail：cjisq@lxdjzypg.parks.cn

1429。姓名: 解立豪

住址（公园）：福建省平潭综合实验区平潭县南继路 565 号歧福公园（邮政编码：299846）。联系电话：65610945。电子邮箱：barvz@qkzwgsef.parks.cn

Zhù zhǐ: Xiè Lì Háo Fújiàn Shěng Píng Tán Zònghé Shíyàn Qū Píng Tán Xiàn Nán Jì Lù 565 Hào Qí Fú Gōng Yuán（Yóuzhèng Biānmǎ：299846). Liánxì Diànhuà：65610945. Diànzǐ Yóuxiāng：barvz@qkzwgsef.parks.cn

Li Hao Xie, Qi Fu Park, 565 Nan Ji Road, Pingtan County, Pingtan Comprehensive Experimental Area, Fujian. Postal Code: 299846. Phone Number：65610945. E-mail：barvz@qkzwgsef.parks.cn

1430。姓名: 毕顺化

住址（博物院）： 福建省漳州市诏安县易翰路 160 号漳州博物馆（邮政编码：274820）。联系电话：94521977。电子邮箱：jrqxs@ekbvzjtd.museums.cn

Zhù zhǐ: Bì Shùn Huā Fújiàn Shěng Zhāngzhōu Shì Zhào Ānxiàn Yì Hàn Lù 160 Hào Zāngzōu Bó Wù Guǎn (Yóuzhèng Biānmǎ：274820). Liánxì Diànhuà：94521977. Diànzǐ Yóuxiāng：jrqxs@ekbvzjtd.museums.cn

Shun Hua Bi, Zhangzhou Museum, 160 Yi Han Road, Zhaoan County, Zhangzhou, Fujian. Postal Code: 274820. Phone Number：94521977. E-mail：jrqxs@ekbvzjtd.museums.cn

1431。姓名: 嵇乙亭

住址（家庭）： 福建省平潭综合实验区平潭县敬星路 247 号翰可公寓 14 层 629 室（邮政编码：792390）。联系电话：63668513。电子邮箱：kmuen@nobltwrp.cn

Zhù zhǐ: Jī Yǐ Tíng Fújiàn Shěng Píng Tán Zònghé Shíyàn Qū Píng Tán Xiàn Jìng Xīng Lù 247 Hào Hàn Kě Gōng Yù 14 Céng 629 Shì (Yóuzhèng Biānmǎ：792390). Liánxì Diànhuà：63668513. Diànzǐ Yóuxiāng：kmuen@nobltwrp.cn

Yi Ting Ji, Room# 629, Floor# 14, Han Ke Apartment, 247 Jing Xing Road, Pingtan County, Pingtan Comprehensive Experimental Area, Fujian. Postal Code: 792390. Phone Number：63668513. E-mail：kmuen@nobltwrp.cn

1432。姓名: 上官冠陆

住址（公园）： 福建省莆田市城厢区锡近路 731 号化游公园（邮政编码：607323）。联系电话：43013944。电子邮箱：zjirs@xqvarhsp.parks.cn

Zhù zhǐ: Shàngguān Guàn Liù Fújiàn Shěng Pútián Shì Chéngxiāng Qū Xī Jìn Lù 731 Hào Huā Yóu Gōng Yuán (Yóuzhèng Biānmǎ：607323). Liánxì Diànhuà：43013944. Diànzǐ Yóuxiāng：zjirs@xqvarhsp.parks.cn

Guan Liu Shangguan, Hua You Park, 731 Xi Jin Road, Chengxiang District, Putian, Fujian. Postal Code: 607323. Phone Number：43013944. E-mail：zjirs@xqvarhsp.parks.cn

1433。姓名: 乜学辙

住址（公司）：福建省南平市建瓯市俊食路 580 号化铁有限公司（邮政编码：114903）。联系电话：14169861。电子邮箱：zysqw@elnizbdu.biz.cn

Zhù zhǐ: Niè Xué Zhé Fújiàn Shěng Nánpíng Shì Jiàn Ōu Shì Jùn Yì Lù 580 Hào Huā Fū Yǒuxiàn Gōngsī (Yóuzhèng Biānmǎ：114903). Liánxì Diànhuà：14169861. Diànzǐ Yóuxiāng：zysqw@elnizbdu.biz.cn

Xue Zhe Nie, Hua Fu Corporation, 580 Jun Yi Road, Jianou City, Nanping, Fujian. Postal Code: 114903. Phone Number：14169861. E-mail：zysqw@elnizbdu.biz.cn

1434。姓名: 第五坚毅

住址（火车站）：福建省龙岩市上杭县葛毅路 216 号龙岩站（邮政编码：569577）。联系电话：19994177。电子邮箱：oegtd@zryvdpal.chr.cn

Zhù zhǐ: Dìwǔ Jiān Yì Fújiàn Shěng Lóngyán Shì Shàng Háng Xiàn Gé Yì Lù 216 Hào Lóngyán Zhàn (Yóuzhèng Biānmǎ：569577). Liánxì Diànhuà：19994177. Diànzǐ Yóuxiāng：oegtd@zryvdpal.chr.cn

Jian Yi Diwu, Longyan Railway Station, 216 Ge Yi Road, Shanghang County, Longyan, Fujian. Postal Code: 569577. Phone Number：19994177. E-mail：oegtd@zryvdpal.chr.cn

1435。姓名: 欧阳智白

住址（火车站）：福建省厦门市同安区继豹路 972 号厦门站（邮政编码：893509）。联系电话：35260754。电子邮箱：djcmp@vdkofrlq.chr.cn

Zhù zhǐ: Ōuyáng Zhì Bái Fújiàn Shěng Xiàmén Shì Tóngān Qū Jì Bào Lù 972 Hào Xiàmén Zhàn (Yóuzhèng Biānmǎ：893509). Liánxì Diànhuà：35260754. Diànzǐ Yóuxiāng：djcmp@vdkofrlq.chr.cn

Zhi Bai Ouyang, Xiamen Railway Station, 972 Ji Bao Road, Tongan District, Xiamen, Fujian. Postal Code: 893509. Phone Number：35260754. E-mail：djcmp@vdkofrlq.chr.cn

1436。姓名: 危领泽

住址（公司）：福建省宁德市古田县葛顺路 930 号恩柱有限公司（邮政编码：279630）。联系电话：34385514。电子邮箱：ghsbc@gufzwsyl.biz.cn

Zhù zhǐ: Wēi Lǐng Zé Fújiàn Shěng Níngdé Shì Gǔtián Xiàn Gé Shùn Lù 930 Hào Ēn Zhù Yǒuxiàn Gōngsī (Yóuzhèng Biānmǎ：279630). Liánxì Diànhuà：34385514. Diànzǐ Yóuxiāng：ghsbc@gufzwsyl.biz.cn

Ling Ze Wei, En Zhu Corporation, 930 Ge Shun Road, Gutian County, Ningde, Fujian. Postal Code: 279630. Phone Number：34385514. E-mail：ghsbc@gufzwsyl.biz.cn

1437。姓名: 华祥冕

住址（公园）：福建省莆田市城厢区桥锤路 198 号超仲公园（邮政编码：272366）。联系电话：39800283。电子邮箱：nkqbz@arewfdzx.parks.cn

Zhù zhǐ: Huà Xiáng Miǎn Fújiàn Shěng Pútián Shì Chéngxiāng Qū Qiáo Chuí Lù 198 Hào Chāo Zhòng Gōng Yuán (Yóuzhèng Biānmǎ：272366). Liánxì Diànhuà：39800283. Diànzǐ Yóuxiāng：nkqbz@arewfdzx.parks.cn

Xiang Mian Hua, Chao Zhong Park, 198 Qiao Chui Road, Chengxiang District, Putian, Fujian. Postal Code: 272366. Phone Number：39800283. E-mail：nkqbz@arewfdzx.parks.cn

1438。姓名: 居自豪

住址（湖泊）：福建省三明市将乐县成翰路 199 号晗智湖（邮政编码：741036）。联系电话：87386287。电子邮箱：limze@exjyzrcb.lakes.cn

Zhù zhǐ: Jū Zì Háo Fújiàn Shěng Sānmíng Shì Jiāng Lè Xiàn Chéng Hàn Lù 199 Hào Hán Zhì Hú (Yóuzhèng Biānmǎ：741036). Liánxì Diànhuà：87386287. Diànzǐ Yóuxiāng：limze@exjyzrcb.lakes.cn

Zi Hao Ju, Han Zhi Lake, 199 Cheng Han Road, Jiangle County, Sanming, Fujian. Postal Code: 741036. Phone Number：87386287. E-mail：limze@exjyzrcb.lakes.cn

1439。姓名: 郝立轶

住址（湖泊）：福建省漳州市云霄县冕克路 295 号焯俊湖（邮政编码：830887）。联系电话：99734430。电子邮箱：cwvzq@lorwafbg.lakes.cn

Zhù zhǐ: Hǎo Lì Yì Fújiàn Shěng Zhāngzhōu Shì Yúnxiāo Xiàn Miǎn Kè Lù 295 Hào Chāo Jùn Hú (Yóuzhèng Biānmǎ：830887). Liánxì Diànhuà：99734430. Diànzǐ Yóuxiāng：cwvzq@lorwafbg.lakes.cn

Li Yi Hao, Chao Jun Lake, 295 Mian Ke Road, Yunxiao County, Zhangzhou, Fujian. Postal Code: 830887. Phone Number：99734430. E-mail：cwvzq@lorwafbg.lakes.cn

1440。姓名: 毕淹己

住址（大学）：福建省莆田市仙游县征禹大学自星路 435 号（邮政编码：153810）。联系电话：11548073。电子邮箱：rezum@qkxwnvdy.edu.cn

Zhù zhǐ: Bì Yān Jǐ Fújiàn Shěng Pútián Shì Xiān Yóu Xiàn Zhēng Yǔ DàxuéZì Xīng Lù 435 Hào (Yóuzhèng Biānmǎ：153810). Liánxì Diànhuà：11548073. Diànzǐ Yóuxiāng：rezum@qkxwnvdy.edu.cn

Yan Ji Bi, Zheng Yu University, 435 Zi Xing Road, Xianyou County, Putian, Fujian. Postal Code: 153810. Phone Number：11548073. E-mail：rezum@qkxwnvdy.edu.cn

CHAPTER 4: NAME, SURNAME & ADDRESSES (91-120)

1441。姓名: 咸祥亚

住址（医院）：福建省莆田市荔城区谢钦路 784 号毅盛医院（邮政编码：353335）。联系电话：87115699。电子邮箱：wgful@htrebfgq.health.cn

Zhù zhǐ: Xián Xiáng Yà Fújiàn Shěng Pútián Shì Lì Chéngqū Xiè Qīn Lù 784 Hào Yì Shèng Yī Yuàn（Yóuzhèng Biānmǎ：353335). Liánxì Diànhuà：87115699. Diànzǐ Yóuxiāng：wgful@htrebfgq.health.cn

Xiang Ya Xian, Yi Sheng Hospital, 784 Xie Qin Road, Licheng District, Putian, Fujian. Postal Code: 353335. Phone Number：87115699. E-mail：wgful@htrebfgq.health.cn

1442。姓名: 卜鸣熔

住址（酒店）：福建省泉州市丰泽区跃晖路 714 号汉进酒店（邮政编码：343018）。联系电话：51525641。电子邮箱：nkxfs@lgqcrvyb.biz.cn

Zhù zhǐ: Bǔ Míng Róng Fújiàn Shěng Quánzhōu Shì Fēng Zé Qū Yuè Huī Lù 714 Hào Hàn Jìn Jiǔ Diàn（Yóuzhèng Biānmǎ：343018). Liánxì Diànhuà：51525641. Diànzǐ Yóuxiāng：nkxfs@lgqcrvyb.biz.cn

Ming Rong Bu, Han Jin Hotel, 714 Yue Hui Road, Fengze District, Quanzhou, Fujian. Postal Code: 343018. Phone Number：51525641. E-mail：nkxfs@lgqcrvyb.biz.cn

1443。姓名: 戈继德

住址（公共汽车站）：福建省宁德市周宁县学源路 254 号奎德站（邮政编码：208200）。联系电话：24021457。电子邮箱：eujmh@phrbwmeo.transport.cn

Zhù zhǐ: Gē Jì Dé Fújiàn Shěng Níngdé Shì Zhōu Níngxiàn Xué Yuán Lù 254 Hào Kuí Dé Zhàn（Yóuzhèng Biānmǎ：208200). Liánxì Diànhuà：24021457. Diànzǐ Yóuxiāng：eujmh@phrbwmeo.transport.cn

Ji De Ge, Kui De Bus Station, 254 Xue Yuan Road, Zhouning County, Ningde, Fujian. Postal Code: 208200. Phone Number：24021457. E-mail：eujmh@phrbwmeo.transport.cn

1444。姓名: 公大九

住址（酒店）：福建省莆田市荔城区禹发路 232 号可敬酒店（邮政编码：683089）。联系电话：73909859。电子邮箱：rjhgv@tlevmqbs.biz.cn

Zhù zhǐ: Gōng Dài Jiǔ Fújiàn Shěng Pútián Shì Lì Chéngqū Yǔ Fā Lù 232 Hào Kě Jìng Jiǔ Diàn（Yóuzhèng Biānmǎ：683089). Liánxì Diànhuà：73909859. Diànzǐ Yóuxiāng：rjhgv@tlevmqbs.biz.cn

Dai Jiu Gong, Ke Jing Hotel, 232 Yu Fa Road, Licheng District, Putian, Fujian. Postal Code: 683089. Phone Number：73909859. E-mail：rjhgv@tlevmqbs.biz.cn

1445。姓名: 滕己嘉

住址（大学）：福建省平潭综合实验区平潭县顺豪大学彬波路 666 号（邮政编码：885128）。联系电话：25222206。电子邮箱：lugkm@dskpiyjo.edu.cn

Zhù zhǐ: Téng Jǐ Jiā Fújiàn Shěng Píng Tán Zònghé Shíyàn Qū Píng Tán Xiàn Shùn Háo DàxuéBīn Bō Lù 666 Hào（Yóuzhèng Biānmǎ：885128). Liánxì Diànhuà：25222206. Diànzǐ Yóuxiāng：lugkm@dskpiyjo.edu.cn

Ji Jia Teng, Shun Hao University, 666 Bin Bo Road, Pingtan County, Pingtan Comprehensive Experimental Area, Fujian. Postal Code: 885128. Phone Number：25222206. E-mail：lugkm@dskpiyjo.edu.cn

1446。姓名: 康振跃

住址（公园）：福建省宁德市柘荣县珏楚路 957 号仲铭公园（邮政编码：625047）。联系电话：55863629。电子邮箱：mfocq@ihukpqmr.parks.cn

Zhù zhǐ: Kāng Zhèn Yuè Fújiàn Shěng Níngdé Shì Zhè Róngxiàn Jué Chǔ Lù 957 Hào Zhòng Míng Gōng Yuán（Yóuzhèng Biānmǎ：625047). Liánxì Diànhuà：55863629. Diànzǐ Yóuxiāng：mfocq@ihukpqmr.parks.cn

Zhen Yue Kang, Zhong Ming Park, 957 Jue Chu Road, Zherong County, Ningde, Fujian. Postal Code: 625047. Phone Number：55863629. E-mail：mfocq@ihukpqmr.parks.cn

1447。姓名: 宇文屹不

住址（广场）：福建省平潭综合实验区平潭县晖王路 534 号食继广场（邮政编码：944407）。联系电话：38331659。电子邮箱：yipel@geqjovix.squares.cn

Zhù zhǐ: Yǔwén Yì Bù Fújiàn Shěng Píng Tán Zònghé Shíyàn Qū Píng Tán Xiàn Huī Wàng Lù 534 Hào Yì Jì Guǎng Chǎng（Yóuzhèng Biānmǎ：944407). Liánxì Diànhuà：38331659. Diànzǐ Yóuxiāng：yipel@geqjovix.squares.cn

Yi Bu Yuwen, Yi Ji Square, 534 Hui Wang Road, Pingtan County, Pingtan Comprehensive Experimental Area, Fujian. Postal Code: 944407. Phone Number：38331659. E-mail：yipel@geqjovix.squares.cn

1448。姓名: 滕石腾

住址（广场）：福建省漳州市东山县辉钦路 568 号刚昌广场（邮政编码：163969）。联系电话：40076911。电子邮箱：dqfgr@zqydlsej.squares.cn

Zhù zhǐ: Téng Dàn Téng Fújiàn Shěng Zhāngzhōu Shì Dōngshān Xiàn Huī Qīn Lù 568 Hào Gāng Chāng Guǎng Chǎng（Yóuzhèng Biānmǎ：163969). Liánxì Diànhuà：40076911. Diànzǐ Yóuxiāng：dqfgr@zqydlsej.squares.cn

Dan Teng Teng, Gang Chang Square, 568 Hui Qin Road, Dongshan County, Zhangzhou, Fujian. Postal Code: 163969. Phone Number：40076911. E-mail：dqfgr@zqydlsej.squares.cn

1449。姓名: 伍启甫

住址（广场）：福建省漳州市龙文区舟队路 670 号领铭广场（邮政编码：321746）。联系电话：11884797。电子邮箱：xueos@vmkspaer.squares.cn

Zhù zhǐ: Wǔ Qǐ Fǔ Fújiàn Shěng Zhāngzhōu Shì Lóng Wén Qū Zhōu Duì Lù 670 Hào Lǐng Míng Guǎng Chǎng（Yóuzhèng Biānmǎ：321746). Liánxì Diànhuà：11884797. Diànzǐ Yóuxiāng：xueos@vmkspaer.squares.cn

Qi Fu Wu, Ling Ming Square, 670 Zhou Dui Road, Longwen District, Zhangzhou, Fujian. Postal Code: 321746. Phone Number：11884797. E-mail：xueos@vmkspaer.squares.cn

1450。姓名: 穆毅南

住址（公司）：福建省平潭综合实验区平潭县化强路 367 号居禹有限公司（邮政编码：535883）。联系电话：69289852。电子邮箱：kbspu@gkdzifha.biz.cn

Zhù zhǐ: Mù Yì Nán Fújiàn Shěng Píng Tán Zònghé Shíyàn Qū Píng Tán Xiàn Huà Qiǎng Lù 367 Hào Jū Yǔ Yǒuxiàn Gōngsī（Yóuzhèng Biānmǎ：535883). Liánxì Diànhuà：69289852. Diànzǐ Yóuxiāng：kbspu@gkdzifha.biz.cn

Yi Nan Mu, Ju Yu Corporation, 367 Hua Qiang Road, Pingtan County, Pingtan Comprehensive Experimental Area, Fujian. Postal Code: 535883. Phone Number：69289852. E-mail：kbspu@gkdzifha.biz.cn

1451。姓名: 陈隆咚

住址（公司）：福建省莆田市荔城区金其路 118 号铁风有限公司（邮政编码：600629）。联系电话：54456187。电子邮箱：mgpna@udmlntkb.biz.cn

Zhù zhǐ: Chén Lóng Dōng Fújiàn Shěng Pútián Shì Lì Chéngqū Jīn Qí Lù 118 Hào Tiě Fēng Yǒuxiàn Gōngsī（Yóuzhèng Biānmǎ：600629). Liánxì Diànhuà：54456187. Diànzǐ Yóuxiāng：mgpna@udmlntkb.biz.cn

Long Dong Chen, Tie Feng Corporation, 118 Jin Qi Road, Licheng District, Putian, Fujian. Postal Code: 600629. Phone Number：54456187. E-mail：mgpna@udmlntkb.biz.cn

1452。姓名: 舒辉钦

住址（湖泊）：福建省宁德市周宁县昌盛路 803 号队仓湖（邮政编码：285672）。联系电话：74582820。电子邮箱：oradb@zwgvmfxs.lakes.cn

Zhù zhǐ: Shū Huī Qīn Fújiàn Shěng Níngdé Shì Zhōu Níngxiàn Chāng Shèng Lù 803 Hào Duì Cāng Hú（Yóuzhèng Biānmǎ：285672). Liánxì Diànhuà：74582820. Diànzǐ Yóuxiāng：oradb@zwgvmfxs.lakes.cn

Hui Qin Shu, Dui Cang Lake, 803 Chang Sheng Road, Zhouning County, Ningde, Fujian. Postal Code: 285672. Phone Number：74582820. E-mail：oradb@zwgvmfxs.lakes.cn

1453。姓名: 邓伦领

住址（博物院）：福建省龙岩市漳平市焯鸣路 776 号龙岩博物馆（邮政编码：351675）。联系电话：28310746。电子邮箱：amosj@mvfobpsy.museums.cn

Zhù zhǐ: Dèng Lún Lǐng Fújiàn Shěng Lóngyán Shì Zhāng Píngshì Chāo Míng Lù 776 Hào Lóngyán Bó Wù Guǎn（Yóuzhèng Biānmǎ：351675). Liánxì Diànhuà：28310746. Diànzǐ Yóuxiāng：amosj@mvfobpsy.museums.cn

Lun Ling Deng, Longyan Museum, 776 Chao Ming Road, Zhangping, Longyan, Fujian. Postal Code: 351675. Phone Number：28310746. E-mail：amosj@mvfobpsy.museums.cn

1454。姓名: 寿智郁

住址（机场）：福建省龙岩市漳平市葆柱路 638 号龙岩坡跃国际机场（邮政编码：165336）。联系电话：16339535。电子邮箱：ycbid@swfijdpo.airports.cn

Zhù zhǐ: Shòu Zhì Yù Fújiàn Shěng Lóngyán Shì Zhāng Píngshì Bǎo Zhù Lù 638 Hào Lóngyán Pō Yuè Guó Jì Jī Chǎng (Yóuzhèng Biānmǎ：165336). Liánxì Diànhuà：16339535. Diànzǐ Yóuxiāng：ycbid@swfijdpo.airports.cn

Zhi Yu Shou, Longyan Po Yue International Airport, 638 Bao Zhu Road, Zhangping, Longyan, Fujian. Postal Code: 165336. Phone Number：16339535. E-mail：ycbid@swfijdpo.airports.cn

1455。姓名: 奚汉员

住址（博物院）：福建省平潭综合实验区平潭县熔茂路 473 号平潭综合实验区博物馆（邮政编码：195371）。联系电话：30553765。电子邮箱：yzrbq@zxvslekm.museums.cn

Zhù zhǐ: Xī Hàn Yuán Fújiàn Shěng Píng Tán Zònghé Shíyàn Qū Píng Tán Xiàn Róng Mào Lù 473 Hào Píng Tán Zòngé íyàn Qū Bó Wù Guǎn (Yóuzhèng Biānmǎ：195371). Liánxì Diànhuà：30553765. Diànzǐ Yóuxiāng：yzrbq@zxvslekm.museums.cn

Han Yuan Xi, Pingtan Comprehensive Experimental Area Museum, 473 Rong Mao Road, Pingtan County, Pingtan Comprehensive Experimental Area, Fujian. Postal Code: 195371. Phone Number：30553765. E-mail：yzrbq@zxvslekm.museums.cn

1456。姓名: 骆伦炯

住址（酒店）：福建省三明市宁化县食不路 252 号世铁酒店（邮政编码：378368）。联系电话：84517191。电子邮箱：bomcv@jlfbeynv.biz.cn

Zhù zhǐ: Luò Lún Jiǒng Fújiàn Shěng Sānmíng Shì Níng Huà Xiàn Shí Bù Lù 252 Hào Shì Tiě Jiǔ Diàn (Yóuzhèng Biānmǎ：378368). Liánxì Diànhuà：84517191. Diànzǐ Yóuxiāng：bomcv@jlfbeynv.biz.cn

Lun Jiong Luo, Shi Tie Hotel, 252 Shi Bu Road, Ninghua County, Sanming, Fujian. Postal Code: 378368. Phone Number：84517191. E-mail：bomcv@jlfbeynv.biz.cn

1457。姓名: 司寇译石

住址（广场）：福建省南平市政和县全近路 122 号稼熔广场（邮政编码：419259）。联系电话：79273663。电子邮箱：esbnm@ecfhozsr.squares.cn

Zhù zhǐ: Sīkòu Yì Dàn Fújiàn Shěng Nánpíng Shì Zhènghé Xiàn Quán Jìn Lù 122 Hào Jià Róng Guǎng Chǎng (Yóuzhèng Biānmǎ：419259). Liánxì Diànhuà：79273663. Diànzǐ Yóuxiāng：esbnm@ecfhozsr.squares.cn

Yi Dan Sikou, Jia Rong Square, 122 Quan Jin Road, Zhenghe County, Nanping, Fujian. Postal Code: 419259. Phone Number：79273663. E-mail：esbnm@ecfhozsr.squares.cn

1458。姓名: 古郁懂

住址（公园）：福建省平潭综合实验区平潭县中陶路 614 号际强公园（邮政编码：937465）。联系电话：47797218。电子邮箱：rivon@bnlfsydt.parks.cn

Zhù zhǐ: Gǔ Yù Dǒng Fújiàn Shěng Píng Tán Zònghé Shíyàn Qū Píng Tán Xiàn Zhōng Táo Lù 614 Hào Jì Qiáng Gōng Yuán (Yóuzhèng Biānmǎ：937465). Liánxì Diànhuà：47797218. Diànzǐ Yóuxiāng：rivon@bnlfsydt.parks.cn

Yu Dong Gu, Ji Qiang Park, 614 Zhong Tao Road, Pingtan County, Pingtan Comprehensive Experimental Area, Fujian. Postal Code: 937465. Phone Number：47797218. E-mail：rivon@bnlfsydt.parks.cn

1459。姓名: 郜计斌

住址（广场）：福建省平潭综合实验区平潭县化红路 689 号翰熔广场（邮政编码：274506）。联系电话：41171780。电子邮箱：luctm@itfnsybe.squares.cn

Zhù zhǐ: Tái Jì Bīn Fújiàn Shěng Píng Tán Zònghé Shíyàn Qū Píng Tán Xiàn Huā Hóng Lù 689 Hào Hàn Róng Guǎng Chǎng (Yóuzhèng Biānmǎ：274506). Liánxì Diànhuà：41171780. Diànzǐ Yóuxiāng：luctm@itfnsybe.squares.cn

Ji Bin Tai, Han Rong Square, 689 Hua Hong Road, Pingtan County, Pingtan Comprehensive Experimental Area, Fujian. Postal Code: 274506. Phone Number：41171780. E-mail：luctm@itfnsybe.squares.cn

1460。姓名: 倪洵亮

住址（湖泊）：福建省南平市延平区俊盛路 355 号鹤山湖（邮政编码：434040）。联系电话：54594856。电子邮箱：imvnj@pfvyblzr.lakes.cn

Zhù zhǐ: Ní Xún Liàng Fújiàn Shěng Nánpíng Shì Yánpíng Qū Jùn Chéng Lù 355 Hào Hè Shān Hú (Yóuzhèng Biānmǎ：434040). Liánxì Diànhuà：54594856. Diànzǐ Yóuxiāng：imvnj@pfvyblzr.lakes.cn

Xun Liang Ni, He Shan Lake, 355 Jun Cheng Road, Yanping District, Nanping, Fujian. Postal Code: 434040. Phone Number：54594856. E-mail：imvnj@pfvyblzr.lakes.cn

1461。姓名: 申屠铭炯

住址（公共汽车站）：福建省漳州市云霄县隆茂路 402 号歧征站（邮政编码：228894）。联系电话：33347339。电子邮箱：pvwft@xamshode.transport.cn

Zhù zhǐ: Shēntú Míng Jiǒng Fújiàn Shěng Zhāngzhōu Shì Yúnxiāo Xiàn Lóng Mào Lù 402 Hào Qí Zhēng Zhàn (Yóuzhèng Biānmǎ：228894). Liánxì Diànhuà：33347339. Diànzǐ Yóuxiāng：pvwft@xamshode.transport.cn

Ming Jiong Shentu, Qi Zheng Bus Station, 402 Long Mao Road, Yunxiao County, Zhangzhou, Fujian. Postal Code: 228894. Phone Number：33347339. E-mail：pvwft@xamshode.transport.cn

1462。姓名: 山兵冕

住址（大学）：福建省莆田市涵江区迅豪大学迅陆路 502 号（邮政编码：249182）。联系电话：51216673。电子邮箱：tspjw@vktozfrm.edu.cn

Zhù zhǐ: Shān Bīng Miǎn Fújiàn Shěng Pútián Shì Hánjiāng Qū Xùn Háo DàxuéXùn Liù Lù 502 Hào（Yóuzhèng Biānmǎ：249182). Liánxì Diànhuà：51216673. Diànzǐ Yóuxiāng：tspjw@vktozfrm.edu.cn

Bing Mian Shan, Xun Hao University, 502 Xun Liu Road, Hanjiang District, Putian, Fujian. Postal Code: 249182. Phone Number：51216673. E-mail：tspjw@vktozfrm.edu.cn

1463。姓名: 隆化超

住址（公司）：福建省宁德市古田县原焯路 222 号辉领有限公司（邮政编码：787227）。联系电话：61554002。电子邮箱：koyxu@hbirmuon.biz.cn

Zhù zhǐ: Lóng Huà Chāo Fújiàn Shěng Níngdé Shì Gǔtián Xiàn Yuán Chāo Lù 222 Hào Huī Lǐng Yǒuxiàn Gōngsī（Yóuzhèng Biānmǎ：787227). Liánxì Diànhuà：61554002. Diànzǐ Yóuxiāng：koyxu@hbirmuon.biz.cn

Hua Chao Long, Hui Ling Corporation, 222 Yuan Chao Road, Gutian County, Ningde, Fujian. Postal Code: 787227. Phone Number：61554002. E-mail：koyxu@hbirmuon.biz.cn

1464。姓名: 裘鹤可

住址（大学）：福建省莆田市城厢区计不大学科院路 232 号（邮政编码：426514）。联系电话：78022655。电子邮箱：bdiqh@bnlxquhy.edu.cn

Zhù zhǐ: Qiú Hè Kě Fújiàn Shěng Pútián Shì Chéngxiāng Qū Jì Bù DàxuéKē Yuàn Lù 232 Hào（Yóuzhèng Biānmǎ：426514). Liánxì Diànhuà：78022655. Diànzǐ Yóuxiāng：bdiqh@bnlxquhy.edu.cn

He Ke Qiu, Ji Bu University, 232 Ke Yuan Road, Chengxiang District, Putian, Fujian. Postal Code: 426514. Phone Number：78022655. E-mail：bdiqh@bnlxquhy.edu.cn

1465。姓名: 广大黎

住址（公司）：福建省宁德市古田县计勇路 773 号涛水有限公司（邮政编码：941093）。联系电话：91775149。电子邮箱：wmjcg@uaictbsk.biz.cn

Zhù zhǐ: Guǎng Dà Lí Fújiàn Shěng Níngdé Shì Gǔtián Xiàn Jì Yǒng Lù 773 Hào Tāo Shuǐ Yǒuxiàn Gōngsī (Yóuzhèng Biānmǎ：941093). Liánxì Diànhuà：91775149. Diànzǐ Yóuxiāng：wmjcg@uaictbsk.biz.cn

Da Li Guang, Tao Shui Corporation, 773 Ji Yong Road, Gutian County, Ningde, Fujian. Postal Code: 941093. Phone Number：91775149. E-mail：wmjcg@uaictbsk.biz.cn

1466。姓名: 蒙帆惟

住址（大学）：福建省南平市政和县渊强大学泽沛路 824 号（邮政编码：750352）。联系电话：66946056。电子邮箱：qbosg@qhpkeynm.edu.cn

Zhù zhǐ: Méng Fān Wéi Fújiàn Shěng Nánpíng Shì Zhènghé Xiàn Yuān Qiǎng Dàxué Zé Pèi Lù 824 Hào (Yóuzhèng Biānmǎ：750352). Liánxì Diànhuà：66946056. Diànzǐ Yóuxiāng：qbosg@qhpkeynm.edu.cn

Fan Wei Meng, Yuan Qiang University, 824 Ze Pei Road, Zhenghe County, Nanping, Fujian. Postal Code: 750352. Phone Number：66946056. E-mail：qbosg@qhpkeynm.edu.cn

1467。姓名: 禄兵昌

住址（火车站）：福建省三明市尤溪县山黎路 903 号三明站（邮政编码：730585）。联系电话：97381888。电子邮箱：puzhr@olprwxtg.chr.cn

Zhù zhǐ: Lù Bīng Chāng Fújiàn Shěng Sānmíng Shì Yóu Xī Xiàn Shān Lí Lù 903 Hào ānmíng Zhàn (Yóuzhèng Biānmǎ：730585). Liánxì Diànhuà：97381888. Diànzǐ Yóuxiāng：puzhr@olprwxtg.chr.cn

Bing Chang Lu, Sanming Railway Station, 903 Shan Li Road, Youxi County, Sanming, Fujian. Postal Code: 730585. Phone Number：97381888. E-mail：puzhr@olprwxtg.chr.cn

1468。姓名: 扈九风

住址（公共汽车站）：福建省龙岩市新罗区斌锤路 406 号启员站（邮政编码：699493）。联系电话：88535707。电子邮箱：kfngt@bsmdpjcl.transport.cn

Zhù zhǐ: Hù Jiǔ Fēng Fújiàn Shěng Lóngyán Shì Xīn Luō Qū Bīn Chuí Lù 406 Hào Qǐ Yún Zhàn（Yóuzhèng Biānmǎ：699493). Liánxì Diànhuà：88535707. Diànzǐ Yóuxiāng：kfngt@bsmdpjcl.transport.cn

Jiu Feng Hu, Qi Yun Bus Station, 406 Bin Chui Road, Silla District, Longyan, Fujian. Postal Code: 699493. Phone Number：88535707. E-mail：kfngt@bsmdpjcl.transport.cn

1469。姓名: 孙坚食

住址（湖泊）：福建省南平市邵武市澜土路 377 号宽祥湖（邮政编码：472580）。联系电话：71625033。电子邮箱：uqvpr@ryxqczaf.lakes.cn

Zhù zhǐ: Sūn Jiān Yì Fújiàn Shěng Nánpíng Shì Shàowǔ Shì Lán Tǔ Lù 377 Hào Kuān Xiáng Hú（Yóuzhèng Biānmǎ：472580). Liánxì Diànhuà：71625033. Diànzǐ Yóuxiāng：uqvpr@ryxqczaf.lakes.cn

Jian Yi Sun, Kuan Xiang Lake, 377 Lan Tu Road, Shaowu, Nanping, Fujian. Postal Code: 472580. Phone Number：71625033. E-mail：uqvpr@ryxqczaf.lakes.cn

1470。姓名: 文锤译

住址（酒店）：福建省南平市武夷山市辉启路 383 号山计酒店（邮政编码：148591）。联系电话：42072467。电子邮箱：ujfix@xckrbwzj.biz.cn

Zhù zhǐ: Wén Chuí Yì Fújiàn Shěng Nánpíng Shì Wǔyíshān Shì Huī Qǐ Lù 383 Hào Shān Jì Jiǔ Diàn (Yóuzhèng Biānmǎ: 148591). Liánxì Diànhuà: 42072467. Diànzǐ Yóuxiāng: ujfix@xckrbwzj.biz.cn

Chui Yi Wen, Shan Ji Hotel, 383 Hui Qi Road, Wuyishan City, Nanping, Fujian. Postal Code: 148591. Phone Number: 42072467. E-mail: ujfix@xckrbwzj.biz.cn

CHAPTER 5: NAME, SURNAME & ADDRESSES (121-150)

1471。姓名: 莘歧昌

住址（博物院）：福建省龙岩市武平县葛计路 523 号龙岩博物馆（邮政编码：145111）。联系电话：79917162。电子邮箱：cilqk@aevbqgxj.museums.cn

Zhù zhǐ: Shēn Qí Chāng Fújiàn Shěng Lóngyán Shì Wǔpíng Xiàn Gé Jì Lù 523 Hào Lóngyán Bó Wù Guǎn (Yóuzhèng Biānmǎ：145111). Liánxì Diànhuà：79917162. Diànzǐ Yóuxiāng：cilqk@aevbqgxj.museums.cn

Qi Chang Shen, Longyan Museum, 523 Ge Ji Road, Wuping County, Longyan, Fujian. Postal Code: 145111. Phone Number：79917162. E-mail：cilqk@aevbqgxj.museums.cn

1472。姓名: 福臻独

住址（公司）：福建省莆田市荔城区强葛路 911 号德威有限公司（邮政编码：669386）。联系电话：63888734。电子邮箱：whabm@fixmpthe.biz.cn

Zhù zhǐ: Fú Zhēn Dú Fújiàn Shěng Pútián Shì Lì Chéngqū Qiáng Gé Lù 911 Hào Dé Wēi Yǒuxiàn Gōngsī (Yóuzhèng Biānmǎ：669386). Liánxì Diànhuà：63888734. Diànzǐ Yóuxiāng：whabm@fixmpthe.biz.cn

Zhen Du Fu, De Wei Corporation, 911 Qiang Ge Road, Licheng District, Putian, Fujian. Postal Code: 669386. Phone Number：63888734. E-mail：whabm@fixmpthe.biz.cn

1473。姓名: 阙汉院

住址（公司）：福建省莆田市仙游县水昌路 263 号冕寰有限公司（邮政编码：629434）。联系电话：62286360。电子邮箱：wtfsi@tsxbpvkw.biz.cn

Zhù zhǐ: Quē Hàn Yuàn Fújiàn Shěng Pútián Shì Xiān Yóu Xiàn Shuǐ Chāng Lù 263 Hào Miǎn Huán Yǒuxiàn Gōngsī (Yóuzhèng Biānmǎ：629434). Liánxì Diànhuà：62286360. Diànzǐ Yóuxiāng：wtfsi@tsxbpvkw.biz.cn

Han Yuan Que, Mian Huan Corporation, 263 Shui Chang Road, Xianyou County, Putian, Fujian. Postal Code: 629434. Phone Number：62286360. E-mail：wtfsi@tsxbpvkw.biz.cn

1474。姓名: 福锤翰

住址（公共汽车站）：福建省三明市尤溪县坡茂路 215 号惟友站（邮政编码：948105）。联系电话：72434607。电子邮箱：blhfv@lunxspkv.transport.cn

Zhù zhǐ: Fú Chuí Hàn Fújiàn Shěng Sānmíng Shì Yóu Xī Xiàn Pō Mào Lù 215 Hào Wéi Yǒu Zhàn (Yóuzhèng Biānmǎ：948105). Liánxì Diànhuà：72434607. Diànzǐ Yóuxiāng：blhfv@lunxspkv.transport.cn

Chui Han Fu, Wei You Bus Station, 215 Po Mao Road, Youxi County, Sanming, Fujian. Postal Code: 948105. Phone Number：72434607. E-mail：blhfv@lunxspkv.transport.cn

1475。姓名: 越员跃

住址（博物院）：福建省厦门市海沧区福员路 376 号厦门博物馆（邮政编码：240749）。联系电话：29222444。电子邮箱：yvrzn@jmlbadvn.museums.cn

Zhù zhǐ: Yuè Yún Yuè Fújiàn Shěng Xiàmén Shì Hǎi Cāng Qū Fú Yún Lù 376 Hào Xiàmén Bó Wù Guǎn (Yóuzhèng Biānmǎ：240749). Liánxì Diànhuà：29222444. Diànzǐ Yóuxiāng：yvrzn@jmlbadvn.museums.cn

Yun Yue Yue, Xiamen Museum, 376 Fu Yun Road, Haicang District, Xiamen, Fujian. Postal Code: 240749. Phone Number：29222444. E-mail：yvrzn@jmlbadvn.museums.cn

1476。姓名: 侯智成

住址（湖泊）：福建省南平市顺昌县己进路 807 号译乙湖（邮政编码：629427）。联系电话：58303175。电子邮箱：axzrk@wfbjshyz.lakes.cn

Zhù zhǐ: Hóu Zhì Chéng Fújiàn Shěng Nánpíng Shì Shùn Chāng Xiàn Jǐ Jìn Lù 807 Hào Yì Yǐ Hú（Yóuzhèng Biānmǎ：629427). Liánxì Diànhuà：58303175. Diànzǐ Yóuxiāng：axzrk@wfbjshyz.lakes.cn

Zhi Cheng Hou, Yi Yi Lake, 807 Ji Jin Road, Shunchang County, Nanping, Fujian. Postal Code: 629427. Phone Number：58303175. E-mail：axzrk@wfbjshyz.lakes.cn

1477。姓名: 桓秀宽

住址（湖泊）：福建省宁德市霞浦县守沛路 783 号亭居湖（邮政编码：225444）。联系电话：34412298。电子邮箱：wnusa@enfomjyg.lakes.cn

Zhù zhǐ: Huán Xiù Kuān Fújiàn Shěng Níngdé Shì Xiápǔ Xiàn Shǒu Pèi Lù 783 Hào Tíng Jū Hú（Yóuzhèng Biānmǎ：225444). Liánxì Diànhuà：34412298. Diànzǐ Yóuxiāng：wnusa@enfomjyg.lakes.cn

Xiu Kuan Huan, Ting Ju Lake, 783 Shou Pei Road, Xiapu County, Ningde, Fujian. Postal Code: 225444. Phone Number：34412298. E-mail：wnusa@enfomjyg.lakes.cn

1478。姓名: 亓官胜可

住址（机场）：福建省泉州市南安市绅敬路 151 号泉州智桥国际机场（邮政编码：289412）。联系电话：44924559。电子邮箱：gqebu@norwtcbz.airports.cn

Zhù zhǐ: Qíguān Shēng Kě Fújiàn Shěng Quánzhōu Shì Nánān Shì Shēn Jìng Lù 151 Hào Quánzōu Zhì Qiáo Guó Jì Jī Chǎng（Yóuzhèng Biānmǎ：289412). Liánxì Diànhuà：44924559. Diànzǐ Yóuxiāng：gqebu@norwtcbz.airports.cn

Sheng Ke Qiguan, Quanzhou Zhi Qiao International Airport, 151 Shen Jing Road, Nanan City, Quanzhou, Fujian. Postal Code: 289412. Phone Number：44924559. E-mail：gqebu@norwtcbz.airports.cn

1479。姓名: 席豹可

住址（湖泊）：福建省三明市三元区桥晗路 570 号兵翰湖（邮政编码：852950）。联系电话：67933427。电子邮箱：vcgtu@ucimdnbe.lakes.cn

Zhù zhǐ: Xí Bào Kě Fújiàn Shěng Sānmíng Shì Sān Yuánqū Qiáo Hán Lù 570 Hào Bīng Hàn Hú (Yóuzhèng Biānmǎ：852950). Liánxì Diànhuà：67933427. Diànzǐ Yóuxiāng：vcgtu@ucimdnbe.lakes.cn

Bao Ke Xi, Bing Han Lake, 570 Qiao Han Road, Sanyuan District, Sanming, Fujian. Postal Code: 852950. Phone Number：67933427. E-mail：vcgtu@ucimdnbe.lakes.cn

1480。姓名: 连绅维

住址（酒店）：福建省泉州市洛江区自世路 458 号食食酒店（邮政编码：738350）。联系电话：80411910。电子邮箱：tgvho@onrcqpbm.biz.cn

Zhù zhǐ: Lián Shēn Wéi Fújiàn Shěng Quánzhōu Shì Luò Jiāng Qū Zì Shì Lù 458 Hào Sì Shí Jiǔ Diàn (Yóuzhèng Biānmǎ：738350). Liánxì Diànhuà：80411910. Diànzǐ Yóuxiāng：tgvho@onrcqpbm.biz.cn

Shen Wei Lian, Si Shi Hotel, 458 Zi Shi Road, Luojiang District, Quanzhou, Fujian. Postal Code: 738350. Phone Number：80411910. E-mail：tgvho@onrcqpbm.biz.cn

1481。姓名: 薄亚亚

住址（公园）：福建省厦门市翔安区敬懂路 513 号员涛公园（邮政编码：250866）。联系电话：38588489。电子邮箱：rwcgd@sfcplqgd.parks.cn

Zhù zhǐ: Bó Yà Yà Fújiàn Shěng Xiàmén Shì Xiáng Ān Qū Jìng Dǒng Lù 513 Hào Yún Tāo Gōng Yuán (Yóuzhèng Biānmǎ：250866). Liánxì Diànhuà：38588489. Diànzǐ Yóuxiāng：rwcgd@sfcplqgd.parks.cn

Ya Ya Bo, Yun Tao Park, 513 Jing Dong Road, Xiangan District, Xiamen, Fujian. Postal Code: 250866. Phone Number：38588489. E-mail：rwcgd@sfcplqgd.parks.cn

1482。姓名: 商顺智

住址（寺庙）：福建省厦门市海沧区秀腾路 414 号陆圣寺（邮政编码：396647）。联系电话：82258840。电子邮箱：iodtr@stykmvpu.god.cn

Zhù zhǐ: Shāng Shùn Zhì Fújiàn Shěng Xiàmén Shì Hǎi Cāng Qū Xiù Téng Lù 414 Hào Liù Shèng Sì（Yóuzhèng Biānmǎ：396647). Liánxì Diànhuà：82258840. Diànzǐ Yóuxiāng：iodtr@stykmvpu.god.cn

Shun Zhi Shang, Liu Sheng Temple, 414 Xiu Teng Road, Haicang District, Xiamen, Fujian. Postal Code: 396647. Phone Number：82258840. E-mail：iodtr@stykmvpu.god.cn

1483。姓名: 於成翰

住址（机场）：福建省厦门市海沧区沛沛路 565 号厦门铁龙国际机场（邮政编码：759501）。联系电话：46066783。电子邮箱：skdof@qkcmdbsw.airports.cn

Zhù zhǐ: Yū Chéng Hàn Fújiàn Shěng Xiàmén Shì Hǎi Cāng Qū Pèi Bèi Lù 565 Hào Xiàmén Tiě Lóng Guó Jì Jī Chǎng（Yóuzhèng Biānmǎ：759501). Liánxì Diànhuà：46066783. Diànzǐ Yóuxiāng：skdof@qkcmdbsw.airports.cn

Cheng Han Yu, Xiamen Tie Long International Airport, 565 Pei Bei Road, Haicang District, Xiamen, Fujian. Postal Code: 759501. Phone Number：46066783. E-mail：skdof@qkcmdbsw.airports.cn

1484。姓名: 宋队浩

住址（博物院）：福建省龙岩市长汀县游泽路 715 号龙岩博物馆（邮政编码：536130）。联系电话：31706484。电子邮箱：ctema@wdeugmzv.museums.cn

Zhù zhǐ: Sòng Duì Hào Fújiàn Shěng Lóngyán Shì Zhǎng Tīng Xiàn Yóu Zé Lù 715 Hào Lóngyán Bó Wù Guǎn（Yóuzhèng Biānmǎ：536130). Liánxì Diànhuà：31706484. Diànzǐ Yóuxiāng：ctema@wdeugmzv.museums.cn

Dui Hao Song, Longyan Museum, 715 You Ze Road, Changting County, Longyan, Fujian. Postal Code: 536130. Phone Number：31706484. E-mail：ctema@wdeugmzv.museums.cn

1485。姓名: 文辙渊

住址（寺庙）：福建省福州市台江区译山路 474 号涛鸣寺（邮政编码：195650）。联系电话：63123237。电子邮箱：snpki@gblpwusz.god.cn

Zhù zhǐ: Wén Zhé Yuān Fújiàn Shěng Fúzhōu Shì Tái Jiāng Qū Yì Shān Lù 474 Hào Tāo Míng Sì（Yóuzhèng Biānmǎ：195650). Liánxì Diànhuà：63123237. Diànzǐ Yóuxiāng：snpki@gblpwusz.god.cn

Zhe Yuan Wen, Tao Ming Temple, 474 Yi Shan Road, Taijiang District, Fuzhou, Fujian. Postal Code: 195650. Phone Number：63123237. E-mail：snpki@gblpwusz.god.cn

1486。姓名: 蓝熔彬

住址（医院）：福建省莆田市仙游县员队路 984 号宽惟医院（邮政编码：721924）。联系电话：38626044。电子邮箱：xkfyu@ucwdeitr.health.cn

Zhù zhǐ: Lán Róng Bīn Fújiàn Shěng Pútián Shì Xiān Yóu Xiàn Yún Duì Lù 984 Hào Kuān Wéi Yī Yuàn（Yóuzhèng Biānmǎ：721924). Liánxì Diànhuà：38626044. Diànzǐ Yóuxiāng：xkfyu@ucwdeitr.health.cn

Rong Bin Lan, Kuan Wei Hospital, 984 Yun Dui Road, Xianyou County, Putian, Fujian. Postal Code: 721924. Phone Number：38626044. E-mail：xkfyu@ucwdeitr.health.cn

1487。姓名: 法易己

住址（医院）：福建省厦门市同安区淹可路 720 号阳阳医院（邮政编码：811136）。联系电话：83359900。电子邮箱：fublz@nvpwqzfx.health.cn

Zhù zhǐ: Fǎ Yì Jǐ Fújiàn Shěng Xiàmén Shì Tóngān Qū Yān Kě Lù 720 Hào Yáng Yáng Yī Yuàn（Yóuzhèng Biānmǎ：811136). Liánxì Diànhuà：83359900. Diànzǐ Yóuxiāng：fublz@nvpwqzfx.health.cn

Yi Ji Fa, Yang Yang Hospital, 720 Yan Ke Road, Tongan District, Xiamen, Fujian. Postal Code: 811136. Phone Number：83359900. E-mail：fublz@nvpwqzfx.health.cn

1488。姓名: 居先科

住址（医院）：福建省莆田市荔城区晗敬路 227 号歧可医院（邮政编码：919161）。联系电话：58519099。电子邮箱：poguy@bhvxcqok.health.cn

Zhù zhǐ: Jū Xiān Kē Fújiàn Shěng Pútián Shì Lì Chéngqū Hán Jìng Lù 227 Hào Qí Kě Yī Yuàn（Yóuzhèng Biānmǎ：919161). Liánxì Diànhuà：58519099. Diànzǐ Yóuxiāng：poguy@bhvxcqok.health.cn

Xian Ke Ju, Qi Ke Hospital, 227 Han Jing Road, Licheng District, Putian, Fujian. Postal Code: 919161. Phone Number：58519099. E-mail：poguy@bhvxcqok.health.cn

1489。姓名: 房队坡

住址（公共汽车站）：福建省南平市邵武市屹陶路 723 号冕计站（邮政编码：429230）。联系电话：38726416。电子邮箱：npldm@drpyvitn.transport.cn

Zhù zhǐ: Fáng Duì Pō Fújiàn Shěng Nánpíng Shì Shàowǔ Shì Yì Táo Lù 723 Hào Miǎn Jì Zhàn（Yóuzhèng Biānmǎ：429230). Liánxì Diànhuà：38726416. Diànzǐ Yóuxiāng：npldm@drpyvitn.transport.cn

Dui Po Fang, Mian Ji Bus Station, 723 Yi Tao Road, Shaowu, Nanping, Fujian. Postal Code: 429230. Phone Number：38726416. E-mail：npldm@drpyvitn.transport.cn

1490。姓名: 邓秀茂

住址（公共汽车站）：福建省平潭综合实验区平潭县郁克路 277 号龙昌站（邮政编码：537997）。联系电话：37070827。电子邮箱：uishe@ihfvzruc.transport.cn

Zhù zhǐ: Dèng Xiù Mào Fújiàn Shěng Píng Tán Zònghé Shíyàn Qū Píng Tán Xiàn Yù Kè Lù 277 Hào Lóng Chāng Zhàn (Yóuzhèng Biānmǎ：537997). Liánxì Diànhuà：37070827. Diànzǐ Yóuxiāng：uishe@ihfvzruc.transport.cn

Xiu Mao Deng, Long Chang Bus Station, 277 Yu Ke Road, Pingtan County, Pingtan Comprehensive Experimental Area, Fujian. Postal Code: 537997. Phone Number：37070827. E-mail：uishe@ihfvzruc.transport.cn

1491。姓名: 井民亚

住址（博物院）：福建省三明市宁化县守德路 352 号三明博物馆（邮政编码：755009）。联系电话：51696623。电子邮箱：ftreg@efvngxyw.museums.cn

Zhù zhǐ: Jǐng Mín Yà Fújiàn Shěng Sānmíng Shì Níng Huà Xiàn Shǒu Dé Lù 352 Hào ānmíng Bó Wù Guǎn (Yóuzhèng Biānmǎ：755009). Liánxì Diànhuà：51696623. Diànzǐ Yóuxiāng：ftreg@efvngxyw.museums.cn

Min Ya Jing, Sanming Museum, 352 Shou De Road, Ninghua County, Sanming, Fujian. Postal Code: 755009. Phone Number：51696623. E-mail：ftreg@efvngxyw.museums.cn

1492。姓名: 蔡宽陆

住址（酒店）：福建省福州市长乐区洵际路 259 号冕轶酒店（邮政编码：322335）。联系电话：42154095。电子邮箱：smbeq@icuryjgv.biz.cn

Zhù zhǐ: Cài Kuān Lù Fújiàn Shěng Fúzhōu Shì Zhǎnglè Qū Xún Jì Lù 259 Hào Miǎn Yì Jiǔ Diàn (Yóuzhèng Biānmǎ：322335). Liánxì Diànhuà：42154095. Diànzǐ Yóuxiāng：smbeq@icuryjgv.biz.cn

Kuan Lu Cai, Mian Yi Hotel, 259 Xun Ji Road, Changle District, Fuzhou, Fujian. Postal Code: 322335. Phone Number：42154095. E-mail：smbeq@icuryjgv.biz.cn

1493。姓名: 姬奎黎

住址（博物院）：福建省漳州市南靖县胜轼路 655 号漳州博物馆（邮政编码：876119）。联系电话：25715512。电子邮箱：grjmk@jogpyiub.museums.cn

Zhù zhǐ: Jī Kuí Lí Fújiàn Shěng Zhāngzhōu Shì Nán Jìng Xiàn Shēng Shì Lù 655 Hào Zāngzōu Bó Wù Guǎn（Yóuzhèng Biānmǎ：876119). Liánxì Diànhuà：25715512. Diànzǐ Yóuxiāng：grjmk@jogpyiub.museums.cn

Kui Li Ji, Zhangzhou Museum, 655 Sheng Shi Road, Nanjing County, Zhangzhou, Fujian. Postal Code: 876119. Phone Number：25715512. E-mail：grjmk@jogpyiub.museums.cn

1494。姓名: 谷愈己

住址（火车站）：福建省龙岩市连城县涛茂路 906 号龙岩站（邮政编码：798582）。联系电话：70499086。电子邮箱：nzlvq@ipjzokec.chr.cn

Zhù zhǐ: Gǔ Yù Jǐ Fújiàn Shěng Lóngyán Shì Liánchéng Xiàn Tāo Mào Lù 906 Hào Lóngyán Zhàn（Yóuzhèng Biānmǎ：798582). Liánxì Diànhuà：70499086. Diànzǐ Yóuxiāng：nzlvq@ipjzokec.chr.cn

Yu Ji Gu, Longyan Railway Station, 906 Tao Mao Road, Liancheng County, Longyan, Fujian. Postal Code: 798582. Phone Number：70499086. E-mail：nzlvq@ipjzokec.chr.cn

1495。姓名: 盖珏大

住址（公共汽车站）：福建省莆田市荔城区仲楚路 266 号豪强站（邮政编码：721214）。联系电话：13807124。电子邮箱：gjpsx@warijqph.transport.cn

Zhù zhǐ: Gài Jué Dà Fújiàn Shěng Pútián Shì Lì Chéngqū Zhòng Chǔ Lù 266 Hào Háo Qiáng Zhàn（Yóuzhèng Biānmǎ：721214). Liánxì Diànhuà：13807124. Diànzǐ Yóuxiāng：gjpsx@warijqph.transport.cn

Jue Da Gai, Hao Qiang Bus Station, 266 Zhong Chu Road, Licheng District, Putian, Fujian. Postal Code: 721214. Phone Number：13807124. E-mail：gjpsx@warijqph.transport.cn

1496。姓名: 郏晖歧

住址（寺庙）：福建省南平市武夷山市咚晗路 887 号钢亚寺（邮政编码：138340）。联系电话：26393373。电子邮箱：fhigt@rsuzwjbh.god.cn

Zhù zhǐ: Jiá Huī Qí Fújiàn Shěng Nánpíng Shì Wǔyíshān Shì Dōng Hán Lù 887 Hào Gāng Yà Sì (Yóuzhèng Biānmǎ：138340). Liánxì Diànhuà：26393373. Diànzǐ Yóuxiāng：fhigt@rsuzwjbh.god.cn

Hui Qi Jia, Gang Ya Temple, 887 Dong Han Road, Wuyishan City, Nanping, Fujian. Postal Code: 138340. Phone Number：26393373. E-mail：fhigt@rsuzwjbh.god.cn

1497。姓名: 蔚译星

住址（博物院）：福建省平潭综合实验区平潭县愈敬路 129 号平潭综合实验区博物馆（邮政编码：647544）。联系电话：61763494。电子邮箱：qphkx@gvtcsmra.museums.cn

Zhù zhǐ: Wèi Yì Xīng Fújiàn Shěng Píng Tán Zònghé Shíyàn Qū Píng Tán Xiàn Yù Jìng Lù 129 Hào Píng Tán Zòngé íyàn Qū Bó Wù Guǎn (Yóuzhèng Biānmǎ：647544). Liánxì Diànhuà：61763494. Diànzǐ Yóuxiāng：qphkx@gvtcsmra.museums.cn

Yi Xing Wei, Pingtan Comprehensive Experimental Area Museum, 129 Yu Jing Road, Pingtan County, Pingtan Comprehensive Experimental Area, Fujian. Postal Code: 647544. Phone Number：61763494. E-mail：qphkx@gvtcsmra.museums.cn

1498。姓名: 南门顺陶

住址（公园）：福建省南平市光泽县队乙路 633 号焯磊公园（邮政编码：620171）。联系电话：71414842。电子邮箱：evghp@wngtuqhr.parks.cn

Zhù zhǐ: Nánmén Shùn Táo Fújiàn Shěng Nánpíng Shì Guāngzé Xiàn Duì Yǐ Lù 633 Hào Zhuō Lěi Gōng Yuán（Yóuzhèng Biānmǎ：620171). Liánxì Diànhuà：71414842. Diànzǐ Yóuxiāng：evghp@wngtuqhr.parks.cn

Shun Tao Nanmen, Zhuo Lei Park, 633 Dui Yi Road, Guangze County, Nanping, Fujian. Postal Code: 620171. Phone Number：71414842. E-mail：evghp@wngtuqhr.parks.cn

1499。姓名: 殳龙兵

住址（寺庙）：福建省厦门市海沧区王豪路 858 号珂风寺（邮政编码：499980）。联系电话：28525864。电子邮箱：urjba@idfkpnlu.god.cn

Zhù zhǐ: Shū Lóng Bīng Fújiàn Shěng Xiàmén Shì Hǎi Cāng Qū Wàng Háo Lù 858 Hào Kē Fēng Sì（Yóuzhèng Biānmǎ：499980). Liánxì Diànhuà：28525864. Diànzǐ Yóuxiāng：urjba@idfkpnlu.god.cn

Long Bing Shu, Ke Feng Temple, 858 Wang Hao Road, Haicang District, Xiamen, Fujian. Postal Code: 499980. Phone Number：28525864. E-mail：urjba@idfkpnlu.god.cn

1500。姓名: 邢稼炯

住址（医院）：福建省厦门市集美区刚强路 564 号友翼医院（邮政编码：808873）。联系电话：35342118。电子邮箱：dxyio@ngljozap.health.cn

Zhù zhǐ: Xíng Jià Jiǒng Fújiàn Shěng Xiàmén Shì Jíměi Qū Gāng Qiǎng Lù 564 Hào Yǒu Yì Yī Yuàn（Yóuzhèng Biānmǎ：808873). Liánxì Diànhuà：35342118. Diànzǐ Yóuxiāng：dxyio@ngljozap.health.cn

Jia Jiong Xing, You Yi Hospital, 564 Gang Qiang Road, Jimei District, Xiamen, Fujian. Postal Code: 808873. Phone Number：35342118. E-mail：dxyio@ngljozap.health.cn

Milton Keynes UK
Ingram Content Group UK Ltd.
UKHW032246291123
433483UK00014B/750

9 798887 554945